D1285410

Raising the Tone of Philosophy

Raising the Tone of Philosophy

Late Essays by Immanuel Kant, Transformative Critique by Jacques Derrida

* * *

Edited by Peter Fenves

The Johns Hopkins University Press
Baltimore and London

Printed in the United States of America on acid-free paper

The Johns Hopkins University Press
2715 North Charles Street
Baltimore, Maryland 21218-4319
The Johns Hopkins Press Ltd., London

Library of Congress Cataloging-in-Publication Data

Raising the tone of philosophy : late essays by Immanuel Kant, transformative critique by Jacques Derrida / edited by Peter Fenves.
p. cm.
Translated from German and French.
Includes bibliographical references and index.
Contents: On a newly arisen superior tone in philosophy : Announcement of a near conclusion of a treaty for eternal peace in philosophy ; Other exaltations / Kant—On a newly arisen apocalyptic tone in philosophy / Derrida.
ISBN 0-8018-4456-8 (hard)
1. Style (Philosophy) I. Kant, Immanuel, 1724–1804. Essays. English. Selections. 1992. II. Derrida, Jacques. D'un ton apocalyptique adopté naguère en philosophie. English. 1992. III. Fenves, Peter D. (Peter David), 1960–
B105.S7R35 1992
193—dc20 92-16600

Contents

Acknowledgments

Without the encouragement of Jacques Derrida, this volume would never have appeared. I also thank John Leavey, Jr., Sam Weber, and Werner Hamacher for their suggestions concerning its scope and content. The staff of the rare books room at the Van Pelt library on the campus of the University of Pennsylvania was exceptionally accommodating in letting me read the works of Johann Georg Schlosser in its possession.

Jacques Derrida, "On a Newly Arisen Apocalyptic Tone in Philosophy," trans. John Leavey, Jr., was first published in *The Oxford Literary Review* 6:2 (1984): 3–37. It is reprinted here in a revised form with the kind permission of the editors.

A Note on the Translation of Kant

The German text on which all translations of Kant are based is *Kants Gesammelte Schriften,* ed. Königliche Preussische (later, Deutsche) Akademie der Wissenschaften (Berlin and Leipzig: Walter de Gruyter, 1902–). Numbers in brackets in the text are the volume and page numbers. I have followed the standard practice and referred to the *Critique of Pure Reason* according to its two original editions: the 1781 one ("A") and the 1787 one ("B"). The notes to Kant's text are indebted to those of Heinrich Maier, editor of the eighth volume of the Akademie edition. I have also profited from the reliable French translation to which Derrida refers, *Première Introduction à la critique de la faculté de juger,* trans. L. Guillermit (Paris: Vrin, 1975). Footnotes in the text are those of the authors, Kant and Derrida; notes at the end of each chapter are those of the translators, Fenves and Leavey, respectively.

The translation of Kant follows more or less established practice. The glossary Werner Pluhar developed for his fine translation of the *Critique of Judgment* (Indianapolis, Ind.: Hackett Publishing Co., 1987) is particularly helpful for the translation of Kant's last writings, and the same is true of the brief glossary Ted Humphrey appended to his translation of Kant's essays on politics and history, *Perpetual Peace and Other Essays* (Indianapolis, Ind.: Hackett Publishing Co., 1983). There is, however, one difficulty in translation that neither Pluhar nor Humphrey—nor indeed any previous translator of Kant—has been forced to resolve, namely the term *vornehm.* In the last section of *Beyond Good and Evil,*

Nietzsche raises the question "Was ist vornehm?" and one can easily refer this question back to the title of the principal Kantian text translated in this volume, "Von einem neuerdings erhobenen vornehmen Ton in der Philosophie." Those who are *vornehm* are taken before all others, hence "preferred"; deference is somehow owed to them. The claim that one is obliged to give preference to certain people and to defer to their wishes even when preference and deference are no longer rooted in hereditary ties to a noble class becomes a focus of attention in Kant's essay. "What is *vornehm?*" turns into a question at the precise historical moment when it is no longer obvious from birth and thus from nature *who* is of high rank in a particular society. Elevation in rank is, however, the key issue in deciding who is *vornehm:* the higher one is, the more one is to be preferred and the less one has to defer to anyone else. For this reason, the word *vornehm* will be translated as "superior." The fact that this word often has sarcastic overtones when applied to so-called distinguished people is not a drawback; indeed, this sarcasm dominates Kant's application of the term *vornehm* to anyone who is not born into the hereditary nobility—and it does not even stop with such upstarts. For any claim to "superiority" counterfeits the claim to "nobility" that all human beings can rightly raise to the extent that it is a "nobility" rooted in their ability to raise themselves above every natu-ability to raise themselves above every natural inclination and thus to become moral agents of the first order.

The present translation differs from other attempts to render Kant into English on at least one score: the word *Schwärmerei* is not translated as "fanaticism." In the highly readable Cambridge edition of Kant's texts on history and politics, the translator, H. B. Nisbet, has noted that "fanaticism" is unsatisfactory (see Kant, *Political Writings,* ed. Hans Reiss, trans. H. B. Nisbet [Cambridge: Cambridge University Press, 1990], 284–85), but his replacement, "zealotry," is no more satisfactory, since the *Schwärmer* whom Kant attacks in his essays are anything but zealous; they are all too phlegmatic. *Schwärmerei* and its many cognates were favorite terms of abuse for Luther, who often employed them in his polemics against "beide papisten und schwermer" (both Papists and *Schwärmer*).

A similar term of abuse developed in English, namely, *enthusiasm.* As *enthusiasm* was used by Schaftesbury and his circle, it captured the ridicule that Luther had unleashed against those who, having lost their senses, claimed direct access to God. But *enthusiasm* has a far nobler heritage than *Schwärmerei;* much of its effectiveness as a term of ridicule derived from the implicit contrast between the modern "enthusiasts" and those whom Plato extolled for their "divine madness." No such ambivalences and ambiguities were possible with the German word, and indeed, the difference between the aims and methods of Luther's polemics and those of Shaftesbury's satires indicates how misleading it would be to translate *Schwärmerei* as "enthusiasm." But there is an even better reason to refrain from this translation: Kant, like other German writers of the eighteenth century, never tired of trying to distinguish a thoroughly repugnant *Schwärmerei* from an *Enthusiasmus* without which "nothing great in the world could take place" (on the history of "enthusiasm," see Peter Fenves, *A Peculiar Fate: Metaphysics and World-History in Kant* [Ithaca, N.Y.: Cornell University Press, 1991], 241–43).

Schwärmerei derives from the swarming of bees. The likeness between the aggregates of swarming bees and the congregations of swarming churchmen gives *Schwärmerei* its highly amorphous and irreducibly figural shape. A commonality between human beings and animals—not human beings and God—is implied in every use of the word. Like bees, *Schwärmer* fly through the air on erratic paths, and, again like bees, they hover there without any easily understood means of support. For this reason, I will translate *Schwärmerei* as "exaltation." Kant indeed interrupts the discourse of his antagonist in order to describe him as an "exalted philosopher" (see 63 below). "Exaltation" is doubtless too positive, too closely connected with an uplifting emotion, but it nevertheless retains a note of danger, of becoming so uplifted that there is no place to go but down. For, as Hölderlin wrote, one can fall upward as well as downward.

Raising the Tone of Philosophy

Introduction: The Topicality of Tone

* * *

Many of Kant's last writings were polemical. After he had announced the completion of his "critical labor" and as he was considering the revisions that were to be elaborated into the *Opus postumum,* he wrote numerous essays and treatises whose very titles often indicated their polemical character. Of all these texts, none is more biting, none more sarcastic, none so wholly satirical as the one written against certain Christianizing Platonists who granted feelings and sentiments a cognitive status. At no other place does Kant go so far as to mimic his antagonists in order to let their words, their attitude, their "attunement"—and so their particular tone—speak for itself. And yet, after an extraordinary display of polemical energy, Kant does not wish to conquer his opponents; rather, he offers them a truce. He has an obligation to make this offer and to avert further philosophical conflict, since his antagonists are not so far removed from the principles and canons of human reason that they would be incapable of coming to terms with the founder of critical philosophy. Once the terms of the truce were fully acknowledged and finally accepted, an "eternal peace" in philosophy could be announced. Such a truce would no doubt promote the basic order of Kantian critical thought—reason above feeling, morality before happiness—but it would nevertheless rest on a common ground shared by all parties to the conflict.

It is all too easy to say that the common ground is human reason itself, not only because Kant himself says no such thing but, above all, because his entire philosophical project had set out to demonstrate the irreducible *complexity* of human reason; to say, on the other hand, that the common ground is a desire for "moral progress" merely indicates the depth of the dispute, since the intractable difference between morality and desire, each of which is "progressive" in its own way, is the very cause of the conflict. The suspicion that the peace treaty from which Kant wishes to exclude no one in principle includes certain hidden clauses whose exact terms cannot be revealed without the treaty at once losing its precise determination and clear destination—this suspicion may have been as much responsible for the refusal on the part of Kant's antagonists to accept the truce as their simple inability or unwillingness to understand the terms he so clearly lays out. One of his antagonists kept up the fight in ever more feeble writings until his death; another soon converted to Catholicism.[1] Their refusal to accept Kant's offer can be seen as a sign that "wars" in philosophy, once again conducted on the famous "battle field" of metaphysics,[2] would take new and unexpected turns. These turns, and the terms in which they are executed, cannot help but raise the topic of tone, since tone defies the stabilization of discourse required to guarantee and even to announce "eternal peace" without equivocation.

Responsibility for this unstable situation is not difficult to find: it is the *possible* inclusion of hidden clauses in a treaty. If there were such clauses in the treaty Kant proposes, the revelation of this secret would immediately undermine its all-inclusive character, and the treaty would at once cease to be a treaty for eternal peace; it would show itself to have been a clandestine means of carrying out an equally underhanded war. For, according to Kant's own widely disseminated proclamations, arcane articles in promises, contracts, or treaties not only violate the unconditional imperative to which every promise, every everlasting accord and every proposal for peace must submit—the imperative that there be no hidden clauses, the transcendental condition that every article in a treaty be out in the open[3]—but, in addition, they do violence to the specific tone in which the "near conclusion" of a treaty for eternal peace alone can be announced: the tone, that is, Kant will call that of "truthfulness" near the conclusion of this very announcement.[4] The revelation of hidden clauses in a treaty is catastrophic, since it destroys the very possibility of peace.

The two dominant senses of *apocalypse,* revelation and destruction, thus merge in this situation, and it is a situation to which every discourse, no matter how well meaning and "open" it may appear, is exposed. For the mere possibility of hidden clauses inhabits every discourse. Jacques Derrida's antipolemical, *grateful* address "On a Newly Arisen Apocalyptic Tone in Philosophy" does not set out to reveal as yet unheard-of clauses or arcane articles in Kant's writing; rather, it undertakes to examine their possibility as an enabling condition on universal communication and "enlightened" discourse in general. The possibility that an announcement hides certain unspoken clauses lies in its *tone;* tonality is, in turn, the preeminent vehicle of catastrophic revelations. To hear tonality otherwise—to write in a tone and of a tone and with a tone *without the key polemical categories of inside and outside,* inclusion and exclusion—is, then, the task of Derrida's address.

Tone is not synonymous with *style.* It is doubtless linked with style insofar as it designates the manner in which a statement is made as opposed to the stated meaning itself, but its own meaning, and its own manner of meaning, is far less stable, far more given to unexpected interruptions and disruptions of, for instance, the very opposition between the manner in which a statement is made and its meaning. For the tone of a discourse is not infrequently precisely its meaning. Not only does tone have a highly determined function in the register of sound and a less clearly defined one in the register of sight; it can also designate an utterly indeterminate and undefinable "atmosphere": the overall arena in which an event takes place. Since the latter sense does not include the distinguishing characteristics of a particular human being, which, since they are absolved from all atmospheric conditions, are more or less fixed, *tone* cannot designate an individual "style." Each tone relates to every other one and to the general field in which this interrelation can take place; none is *sui generis,* each being only a variation of the others. What varies in general is simple enough to state: it is the kind and frequency of *vibration.* In contrast to the punctual performance of the stylus and of style, tone is always somehow vibrant. A *tonos* ("chord") was stretched and strained to the point where it could sustain a distinct vibration, and the resulting sound of this straining blended with more unwieldy noises, in particular, the "din" (*don*) that could be heard in Germanic languages and the "thunder" (*tonare*) that was heard in Latinate ones. Even the etymology of the word *tone* thus gives evidence of a certain instability and vibrancy.[5] The modes and periods of vibration change from one register of usage to the next, but a period, and therefore a specific temporality, marks every tone. Certain vibrations, as ground-shaking tremors, can even set the mind itself into motion. The "emotions" that correspond to these vibrations are themselves tonal; they are the various *Stimmungen,* the moods or dispositions, that respond to a sometimes silent but always vibrant voice (*Stimme*). Kant, like many of his contemporaries, first touches upon the topic of tone in this context.

It is not the vibrations of the air registered by the ear but rather the chronic tremblings of the mind that receive Kant's initial attention. Such tremblings unleash "emotive" vibrancies that are themselves constitutive of an unearthly speech or language (*Sprache*), and this speech or language lets the topic of tone arise in an arena no longer dominated by recognizable and knowable mathematical proportions among vibrating chords. The chronic vibrations to which the human mind is exposed make themselves known with the greatest clarity, moreover, at the precise moment that cognitive discourse—"mathematical" language in a broad sense—exhausts itself. One need not turn to Kant's *Critiques* to find indices of such lateral disturbances, for they traverse his early work and perhaps even dictate the shape of his later, critical labor. Indeed, one *needs* a critique of our cognitive capacities in order to determine the breadth and length of the tremors to which the mind is exposed. In Kant's early writings, unearthly vibrancy during "universal calm" comes to disclose a tonal dimension of a discourse that is otherwise consigned entirely to cognition. Not only is the divine plan revealed as a result of this disclosure, but human beings who are capable of hearing this dimension of discourse become aware of their role in the cosmos at large and their destination after the destruction of their bodies and even of the entire planet: "During the universal stillness of nature and the resting of the senses, the concealed cognitive capacity [*das verborgene Erkenntnisvermögen*] of immortal spirit speaks [*redet*] an unnamable language [*unnennbare Sprache*] and gives many undeveloped concepts that can certainly be felt but cannot be described."[6] The stillness of the night makes room for another kind of vibration, another speech and another language in which the human mind, whose fragility and vulnerability Kant has just taken great pains to describe, is set into motion; the "emotional" character of this experience corresponds to the eruption of this nonearthly, nonphysical vibration. As the divine plan is revealed in this language of "emotion," discourse itself alters; it loses the two principal pillars of its discourse: names and predication. "An unnamable language," which is withdrawn from the domain of description, no longer services cognition, and so Kant has no choice but to latch onto "sentiments" (*Empfindungen*) in order to describe an inexplicable dimension of the faculty of knowledge and cognitive discourse in general. The "concepts" of this language defy analysis and even elude communication if the latter is defined in terms of intersubjective interaction on the basis of common terms. A language without names, predicates, and analyzable concepts is not a language like any other; it can make itself audible only when there is a "universal stillness," when every object of possible knowledge—all of nature, including the mind as a natural object—has ceased to vibrate. Such a language, which is always a matter of "passion" and never a question of action, is pure intonation: the announcement, that is, of complete revelation. Revelation reaches its completion at the very moment the entire cosmos has fallen into ruins.[7] The intonation of cognitive discourse—this newly arisen voice or language of "immortal spirit"—thus announces nothing less than full revelation in cosmic destruction: an apocalypse, in short. During this apocalyptic announcement, the human soul hears of its own survival and feels in its highly strained sinews the vibrations of a higher life, the "immortal" life of "spirit."

Little of this survives the intricate analysis, measurement, and delimitation of the human faculty of cognition undertaken in the *Critique of Pure Reason.* No longer does Kant's exposition of the cognitive faculty invoke an unnamable language whose indescribable concepts defy analysis. If the precise procedure whereby concepts are schematized remains, as Kant declares, "a concealed art in the depths of the human soul" (A 141; B 180) and if, therefore, a key dimension of our cognitive faculty defies philosophical exposition, this awkward situation does not call for the invocation of another mode of human vibrancy, another voice or language, that would somehow be at work in the art of schematization. Not only does his exposition of the specific procedures necessary for human cognition *not* imply a language of divine revelation; it precludes such a language to the extent that its very point is to determine why such a language would have nothing determinate to say, why it would not be a language of cognition and would not even be a *language* in service of reason. But Kant does not therefore abandon all talk of "an unnamable language" that could be heard at the precise point where the cognitive faculty exhausts itself. This language makes itself known, not surprisingly, at the moment the "whole universe" once again threatens to "sink into the abyss of nothingness" (A 622; B 650), and it is here that the topic of tone erupts into a discourse now committed to the thoroughgoing and fundamental critique of the cognitive faculty.

In the section of the Transcendental Dialectic devoted to the demonstration that the "physicotheological proof" of God's existence does not accomplish what it promises, a language unlike all others arises, and this newly exposed language thwarts the threat of losing all support for a potentially vertiginous gaze up into the heavens: "The present world discloses to us so immeasurable [*unermeßlichen*] a stage of variety, order, purposiveness, and beauty . . . that even with such knowledge as our weak understanding can acquire of it, we are brought face to face with so many marvels immeasurably great, that all language [*alle Sprache*] misses [*vermissen*] its force, all numbers their power to measure [*messen*], our thoughts themselves their limitations, so that our judgment of the whole must dissolve into a languageless but, for that reason, all the more persuasive astonishment [*ein sprachloses, aber desto beredteres Erstaunen*]" (A 622; B 650). All language has been lost, and yet something of language, or another language altogether, survives to support a gaze upward: *Beredsamkeit,* eloquence, persuasiveness. The art of this mode of *Rede* (discourse, speech) has traditionally been called "rhetoric"; its aim has always been to hold sway over emotions. Since, however, language has lost its force and every "art"—whether it be that of schematization, counting, or thinking—has concomitantly lost its appropriate measure, the persuasiveness of this "rhetoric" cannot be an arbitrary one; it is not a matter of arbitration or manipulation, and so it is understood to be *necessary:* our judgment must dissolve into the rhetoric of astonishment, a "pathology" in the original sense of the term. No speech could manipulate this pathological condition because the very ability to use language has been lost. And yet, this unique loss of linguistic power, according to a model already familiar to Kant under the term *sublime,*[8] amounts to a gain: an utterly useless language, a language of sheer pathos, a pathology without pain is disclosed. Above all, this language cannot be used to demonstrate the existence of a perfect, divine creator or even to persuade anyone to believe in the existence of such an entity. For to use this language is immediately to lose it, and yet every use of language, indeed every effort at counting or thinking, remains indebted to it to the extent that it alone has the power to thwart the threat of falling into an "abyss of nothingness."

But the very uselessness of this language exposes it to all sorts of dogmatic uses. Kant points out how this rhetoric of astonishment can relieve speculation of the "ponderous indecisiveness" (A 624; B 652) toward which it is naturally impelled. But the rhetoric of astonishment can be decisive precisely because it leaves no room for discussion; nothing can be spoken *of* this language without it becoming something else altogether: an argumentative tool or a discursive procedure. The topic of tone explicitly arises in response to precisely this untenable linguistic situation: the undiscussable, nondiscursive, and decisive moment enters into a discussion and indeed must enter into discussion, but this very entrance involves a mixture of languages and a medley of voices. *The ineluctable plurality of languages and voices gives rise to the topic of tone,* a plurality that is not a mere aggregate of homogeneous languages or voices, each of which would derive from the same source. For the rhetoric of astonishment, this newly overheard language of an outstanding pathos, is incommensurable with the language of measurement, schematization, counting, cognition, and representational thought in general. And yet, the incommensurability of this linguistic plurality itself demands a measure of moderation, a modicum, or, to use Kant's term, a *Mäßigung*—the "toning down," that is, of discourse in general: "it can do no harm to the good cause [*der guten Sache*] to tone down [*herabzustimmen*] dogmatic language of a high-speaking sophist until it reaches the tone of moderation and modesty [*Ton der Mäßigung und Bescheidenheit*], the tone of a belief sufficient for making one quiet but not one that commands absolute submission" (A 624–25; B 653–54).

The topic of tone arises when language neither serves cognition nor imposes an obligation. For the rhetoric of astonishment, which "must" arise, is without a cognitive function and without an ability to command. It necessarily "speaks," but when it is spoken of, when it enters into discussion, it is lost, and the discussion, as a result, is deprived of a clearly delimited topic. Without the possibility of delimitation, critical discourse itself has reached its own limit. Since, however, every discussion is indebted to the rhetoric of astonishment to the extent that it rescues observation and speculation from "ponderous indecisiveness," every discussion encounters this threat: the topic becomes muddled and, in the end, empty; the discussion, in turn, becomes more like idle talk than genuine dialogue. The apotheosis of this idleness in language is the "high-speaking" of dogmatic language. Language has flown so high that it has no clear topic on which it could base a discussion. In order to save discussion from this threat—a threat no less dangerous than that of falling into the "abyss of nothingness" or into "ponderous indecisiveness"—Kant recommends a lower tone, and yet he is unable to specify a standard of measure for tone itself. In the regulation of tone, a measure for incommensurable languages is discovered, but this act of measuring, this moderation, this modulation, or making of a modicum (*Mäßigung*), is itself without a definable measure.[9] The emergence of the topic of tonality registers the eruption of a "space" in which incommensurable languages and incomparable voices encounter one another, and the measure of this incommensurable topic is to be found nowhere but in the "measuring," the moderation or the modulation of tone itself.

"Toning down" a discourse does not simply consist in altering its claims from apodictic ones to hypothetical ones; rather, it involves making room for claims (*Ansprüche*) of necessity that are not apodictic in the traditional sense, since they defy demonstration. In this always indeterminate space, the topic of tone has to arise. Since, however, it is a space traversed by incomparable modes of necessitation, it is a necessarily disputed topic, perhaps the very space of future philosophical disputation. Once it has been disclosed, no one can foreclose further dispute with the conclusive claim *quod est demonstratum;* it therefore remains always open, itself always a matter of dispute. Whether a tone has arisen cannot be answered in the same manner that one can answer a question concerning a possible object of cognition; its "existence" is as indemonstrable as that of a divinity. If, however, revelation is understood as a final demonstration—of things themselves, including God and the immortal soul—then the topic of tone everywhere defies revelation, even as it is implied in every revelatory discourse. In the wake of the *Critique*'s destruction of all possible demonstrations of God's existence, the topic of tone can thus come to designate the very "battle field" on which philosophical disputations will henceforth take place. And Kant himself acknowledges as much in the section of the *Critique* devoted to the polemical employment of pure reason: "That which has become disputable [*streitig*] here is not the subject-matter but rather the tone [*nicht die Sache, sondern der Ton*]" (A 744; B 772).

The conflict over the good cause (*die gute Sache*) is no longer a matter of the thing itself (*die Sache selbst*) but henceforth a matter of tone, and so the dispute, for Kant, comes down to this: since the "language of knowing" (A 745; B 773) has to be "given up," the demonstration of God's existence gives way to a presentation of the indemonstrable in the proper intonation of cognitive discourse. The only appropriate tone where one cannot speak properly of things in themselves is called a "low" one: a tone that does not give rise to an illusion of knowledge. Tone is, in turn, not a thing over which one can dispute but is the dispute itself, a space of conflict emptied of all determinate subject matter. "There should be, properly speaking, no polemic of pure reason," Kant concludes: "For how can two persons carry on a dispute about a thing the reality of which neither of them can present in actual or even in possible experience?" (A 750; B 778). Once the *Critique* has shown the impossibility of divine revelation or rational demonstration of things themselves, no dispute in the field of pure reason properly speaking can rise, and so the merely tonal dispute—the dispute over tone and the dispute as tone—is not, properly speaking, a dispute at all: it is, instead, a figural dispute, a dispute over figures, a dispute without a properly defined field of disputation because every "battle field" of dispute generates more and more figures. Once again, a rhetorical dimension of language emerges, but it is no longer linked to the emotional character of speaking or even to a purely "emotive" language; it is now the necessarily figural dimension of cognitive language. Tone is still in dispute after pure reason has been subject to a thoroughgoing critique, but the very meaning of *dispute* and the modes of establishing its meaning are themselves suspended; the word no longer can refer to a determinate phenomenon but, instead, vibrates as much as the "thing" it is supposed to mean. In the context of a philosophy whose only measure is secure knowledge of objects, there can be no dispute, and yet "disputes" nevertheless live on, and the place of this improper after-battle is precisely "tone." No wonder the term *tone* itself has been displaced from its easily recognizable and highly determinate position in the register of aural sensation and has, as a result, undertaken the task of designating an insensible—unmeasurable if not immense—dimension of discourse. The term thus traverses the cleft separating the sensible from the intelligible. Nevertheless—or precisely for this reason—tone is the very topic of coming "disputes." And one need go no further than the *Critique of Pure Reason* to find the effects of this nearly exposed, measureless space. The complex figural networks of the text take their point of departure from an immense metaphysical "battle field" without blood and an immeasurable "sea" of metaphysical illusions without water.[10]

"Keep the tone down"; this imperative does not imply that there should be no tone at all. Tone has to arise, and its arrival is nothing other than the exposure of an irreducible tonality of cognitive discourse: a purely "emotional" language has emerged in the failure of cognitive discourse, on the one hand, and necessarily improper terms have defined the space of future disputations, on the other. The imperative thus amounts to this: keep rhetoricity in its place, and the name of its place is precisely "tone." If one only knew what this term meant, the imperative could henceforth keep conflict to a minimum. But the very elasticity of the term guarantees that it reserves the possibility of continued conflict. That tone is always implicated in specific modes of vibration and vibrancy has already been indicated. This characteristic is of particular significance when the figural character of the "dispute" over tone is no longer an easy matter to resolve: when, that is, the "dispute" cannot be clearly distinguished from a genuine conflict or even a real war. Such a potentially undecidable moment, which demands decision after decision, emerges whenever the very foundations of the "common essence"—the *Gemeinwesen* or the commonweal—become vibrant, "shaking" (A 749; B 777) as a result of having lost their moorings in divine legitimation. To protect the "common essence" from this shaking and, in turn, to keep the dispute from breaking out into a battle, the following prescription has been delivered: "further the good cause [*die gute Sache*] through sophistical arguments rather than allow its supposed antagonists the advantage of having made us lower our tone to the modicum of mere practical conviction" (A 749; B 777). A heightened tone might secure victory for the "cause," but it would at the same time turn the "dispute" over tone into an actual dispute over a "thing," *die Sache selbst.* A modulation in tone reveals its potential to turn a "dispute" into a dispute and a "dispute" into a dispute, and to do the same with every word. Tonal modulation can do this turning back and forth not because it reveals something, least of all the "highest" thing, but because it can hide vacuity, emptiness, idleness; not only does it reveal nothing, but it can even hide a certain "nothingness" whose name in the context of the legitimation of the common space for social interaction is, quite properly, "illusory grounds." A modulation in tone then puts the entire discourse at risk: it turns into a battleground every bit as real as the battleground over the future constitution of the commonweal. Being aware of such modulations (of lower tone into a higher one, of a dispute into a "dispute," and so forth) becomes the very task of philosophy after all its apparent battles have been played out.

The very fact of tone, no matter how low it might be, retains the possibility of a concealment without retaining the possibility of revelation; even the most minimal tone includes the possibility of hiding its own emptiness, idleness, "nothingness." Since, moreover, there *must be* tone, since its facticity is undeniable and its modulation is always a possibility, such concealment can never be ruled out. And it can thus emerge as the very salvation of philosophy: that which keeps philosophical disputation from the "sleep of death" to which Kant refers in the central article of his "Announcement of the Near Conclusion of a Treaty for Eternal Peace in Philosophy."[11] The emptiness of tone keeps philosophy alive by keeping it awake—to "tone," to "rhetoric," to the unruly difference between the lexical usage of a word and its suspended usage. Philosophy no longer adjudicates disputes but rather, having shown all disputes over "the thing" or "the cause" to be empty, listens to "tones," each of which traverses the cleft separating sensibility from intelligibility. "Tone" is, if it exists at all, the irreducible site of coming "disputes" whose very persistence after the resolution of all genuine conflicts makes the announcement of "eternal peace" into a necessarily ironic one: the announcement that cannot proclaim what it intends to proclaim, namely "eternity" and "peace." No future philosophy can fail to hear this ironic tone.

The treaty for eternal peace in philosophy is always only near, never concluded; it is merely announced, and always announced in a particular tone: that of truthfulness. Listening for tones henceforth constitutes the interminable task of philosophy, a task, moreover, to which philosophy must submit itself after it, having solved the problems first posed by Pythagoras and Plato, has come to a satisfactory conclusion. Whether the topic of tone does not itself disturb the conclusive announcement is a problem—although perhaps not a "philosophical" one—that is both expressed and suppressed in Kant's last writings. The systematic exposition of the metaphysics of morals and the demonstration of a "transition" from the metaphysics of nature to physics itself were the strictly philosophical projects Kant intended to complete after having finished the third and last *Critique,* but neither of these projects was to break any new ground; they were both explications of the "metaphysical" or "dogmatic" implications of the critical works. What Kant did broach in the 1790s was a catalogue of tonal variations. If he did not, as Hölderlin would soon do,[12] work out a "doctrine" of such variations, he nevertheless lays the groundwork for one: each tone of discourse corresponds to a certain "mood" that, in turn, varies according to the exclusivity of the discussion. The livelier the tone, the less prone the mind is to fall into the "sleep of death," but the higher the tone, the more prone the mind is to reduce the possible scope of the discussion and thus to induce the "death" of all philosophy. For each decrease in the degree of life is based on an exclusion of "liveliness" in future discussion. Each of Kant's tones—dogmatic, historical, superior, veridical—belongs to the scale of discursive *vitality,* and tone becomes an immense and immeasurable topic of philosophical discussion at the precise moment when thought is threatened with the two "deaths": the death of "sleep," on the one hand, and the death of "visionary dreaming," on the other.

Hearing tones, which is indissociable from paying attention to the dispositional and rhetorical character of every discourse, names the task of thinking in the future, and tone turns into the unavoidable topic of any thought that can survive these two "deaths." The variety of tones owes its origins to the variety of possible relations to the "life" and "death" not precisely of reason, nor even of rational discourse, but of language in service of reason: a "dogmatic" tone[13] arises whenever statements exclude rational evaluation; a "historical tone"[14] arises whenever statements do not allow for rational evaluation; a "superior tone"[15] arises whenever statements rise above communicative language altogether; a "veridical tone,"[16] by contrast, arises whenever thoughts held in reserve do not contradict any spoken statement and, in addition, whenever reservations concerning the certainty of a statement are not held back. The veridical tone responds and corresponds to an apodictic command ("Do not lie") because it is the one tone that measures up to an unexpected but nevertheless unconditioned imperative: there must be a tone; no thought held in reserve is allowed to escape its linguistic expression. The exclusion of duplicity implies the unacceptability of all "mental reservations," all efforts at withdrawing thought from expression and preserving mental states from language.[17] Each of the other tones violates this newly articulated imperative to the extent that they all hold thought in reserve, disengage thinking from language, and thus condemn themselves at a decisive moment if not to silence, then at least to muteness or infantilism. A veridical tone alone lives up to this imperative and, by so doing, keeps philosophy alive in everlasting "disputes" over "tone" itself. Tone, this word so closely associated with music, not rational discourse, can assume these lifesaving duties because it belongs neither to the domain of spontaneous thought nor simply to receptive sensibility, however pertinent it may be to both.

There must be tone. Silence, to say nothing of muteness or infantilism, will not suffice; indeed, it will lull human reason once again into the "sleep of death." Because tone has the power to awaken—and indeed to awaken Pythagoras, the first philosopher whom we can call a philosopher[18]—tone must remain despite every effort to reduce the rhetorical character of philosophical writing to insignificance. Such is the unexpected imperative that arises out of the completion of Kant's critical labors. Yet the necessity of tone cannot be easily consigned to any of the modes of necessitation Kant had previously uncovered. Since every tone, as the *Critique of Judgment* had determined, corresponds with affective modifications of the mind,[19] the necessity of tone implies a necessary "feeling." If, as the remark in the *Critique of Pure Reason* on the "languageless but, for that reason, all the more persuasive astonishment" suggests, such necessity is only a matter of "pragmatic anthropology," it must be remembered that the principal *pragmata* are no longer the life and death of rational creatures but are, instead, the "life" and "death" of rational discourse, indeed the "life" and "death" of language in service of reason; each of the subsequent critiques did indeed discover a "feeling" whose necessity is not comprehensible according to any anthropological characteristic: the moral feeling of respect, on the one hand, and the aesthetic feelings of beauty and sublimity, on the other. The imperative through which one might be tempted to comprehend the peculiar necessity of tone ("There must be discourse capable of discussion") is, moreover, not one imperative among others; it is the very imperative of reason, the transformation of the principle of sufficient reason into a command that makes possible a proper ordering of both experience and action. But this imperative is insufficiently formulated insofar as it elides its "emotional" dimension: the dimension, that is, in which cognition is itself suspended. The necessity of tone announces itself in another, more complicated imperative: that there must be an ability to communicate, and this ability is itself purely "emotive," never motivational. The necessity of this ability cuts across every previous critical distinction: it does not belong to the conditions in which cognition becomes possible, nor to the self-sufficient motivational force of practical reason, nor even to the necessity claimed in aesthetic judgments, although it is, to be sure, implicated in each of these modes of necessitation. If the statement that there must be the possibility of communication sounds like the basis of a "universal pragmatics,"[20] it is only because the term *pragmatics* designates by default a field in which the necessity of tone finds its home. But this mode of necessity is as difficult to integrate into a program for "pragmatics" as into the program of research for any of the domains capable of a transcendental exposition. For it, once again, cuts across a distinction by which the pragmatic is separated from the aesthetic, the moral, and the cognitive: tonality is applicable not only to discourse capable of mutual comprehension and consent but also, of course, to "incomprehensible" sounds. Since tonality traverses the fundamental distinction between sensibility and intelligibility as its necessity likewise cuts across the distinctions that divide the *Critiques*, its field of application is necessarily unstable and its peculiar necessity cannot be integrated into other, more familiar ones.

So decisively does tone cut across the distinctions developed in the *Critiques* that it eludes the most basic one of all: the distinction between form and matter. No "formal idealism," as Kant would sometimes call his doctrine,[21] can do without this distinction, and every one of the *Critiques* attests to its power: the first one exposes the formal conditions of cognition; the second one, the formulas for purely rational action; the third one, the formality of reflective judgment. But as the *Critique of Judgment* makes clear, tones are at once the matter of certain sensations and the form of certain sensible effects on the mind. The complications in which the final *Critique* entwines itself whenever it tries to resolve this difficulty are immense; they attest to the ability of this one topic of discussion to unravel every distinction deployed to stabilize its infectious vibrancy. When Kant tries to "elucidate by examples" the distinction between pure and empirical judgments of taste,[22] tones occupy a remarkably uncertain position:

> Most people will declare a mere color, such as the green of a lawn, or a mere tone (as distinct from sound and noise), as for example that of a violin, to be beautiful in themselves, even though both seem to be based merely on the matter of presentations, i.e., solely on sensation, and hence only deserve to be called agreeable. And yet it will surely be noticed at the same time that sensations of color as well as of tone claim to deserve being considered beautiful only insofar as they are *pure*. (*CJ*, 70; 5:224)

Kant tries to resolve this dilemma by recalling that tones are "vibrations of the air" and therefore "would not be mere sensations but would already be the formal determination of the manifold of these, in which case they [tones and colors] could even be themselves considered beauties" (*CJ*, 71; 5:224). Not only do the subjunctive verbs indicate the tentativeness and insufficiency of this solution; so too does the proposed resolution in which form and matter are themselves suspended in favor of a certain uniformity: "But what we call pure in a simple kind of sensation is its uniformity, undisturbed and uninterrupted by an alien sensation. It pertains only to form, because there we can abstract from the quality of the kind of sensation in question (as to which color or tone, if any, is presented)" (*CJ*, 71; 5:224). This invocation of uniformity is doubtless meant only to rescue primary colors from an otherwise automatic condemnation to the status of the agreeable and therefore to show how the transcendental exposition of beauty squares with the opinions of "most people," but since it also concerns tone it ends up with this proposal: the uniformity of a vibration in the air deserves to be called beautiful without regard to which tone, if any, it constitutes; silence, as the complete abstraction from all tones, is alone capable of such uniformity, but silence is itself without form. Such minor difficulties grow into ever greater ones every time the topic of tone surfaces in the third *Critique*, and each attempt to bring this topic into clearly defined borders only further disturbs and interrupts the overall presentation.

Nowhere is this topic more disruptive than in the section of the final *Critique* "on the division of the fine arts." Kant himself insists that it is an interruption of his own theory of aesthetic judgment, but it is—and this is once again decisive—a necessary interruption. His effort at separating and dividing the arts, whose very name suggests articulation and division, can claim no other status than a mere projection (*Entwurf*); it is intended not as a theory but only as "one of a variety of attempts [*Versuchen*] that can and should [*soll*] still be made" (*CJ*, 190; 5:321). Since each attempt undertaken under the direction of this imperative will be as preliminary as his own, no attempt will reach its aim: a survey, that is, of decisively divided arts. And so the hitherto dominant aim and intention of dividing, "theory," will no longer guide the undertaking at all; instead, divisions will be projected without theoretical guidance and thus without an idea of the whole. If "analogy" still guides the division Kant himself projects ("the analogy between the arts and the way people express themselves in speech so as to communicate with one another as perfectly as possible" [*CJ*, 189: V, 320]), it is because analogy itself marks an end to logicotheoretical undertakings and indeed to the very one he himself is undertaking in the critique of aesthetic judgment.[23] Tone, as the final category, seals the analogy between speech and art but at the same time makes this division untenable and the process of dividing interminable.

Defined as the "ratio in the varying degrees of attunement (tension) of the sense to which the sensations belong" (*CJ*, 193; 5:324–25), tone comes to determine not only sounds but also, once again, colors. But "tones"—the word now has to take refuge into quotation marks, having become a "term of art"—are more accurately presented as an undecidable addition to cognition, indeed the surplus beyond cognition that does not submit itself to the critique of the *logos* to the precise extent that it eludes decision: "It is worthy of note that these two senses, besides having whatever receptivity for impressions they require in order to obtain concepts of external objects by means of these [senses], are also capable of [having] a special sensation connected with that receptivity, a sensation about which it is difficult to decide whether it is based on sense or reflection" (*CJ*, 193–94; 5:324).[24] The critique of aesthetic judgment is itself based on this distinction between sense and reflection, and it is impossible to execute without an ability to decide on the reflective character of a judgment about sensations. So tentative is the attempt to project a stable division on the basis of an analogy of art to the most perfect possible communication that Kant has to invoke a peculiar mode of necessitation merely to leave the project unresolved and not declare it unresolvable, to leave this project and perhaps more than this project, in other words, for the future: "If we consider all this, one may see oneself compelled [*so möchte man sich genötigt sehen*] to look at [*anzusehen*] sensation of color and tone not as mere sense impressions but as the effect of a judgment of form found in the play of many sensations" (*CJ*, 194; 5:324, translation modified). The compulsion to see oneself see, for example, colors as "tones" and to see, for example, tones as already (subconsciously if not unconsciously) reflective does not simply owe its origin to reflection on oneself nor simply to the inability to carry out this self-reflection to its end; the surprising compulsion to see oneself see colors as "tones" and tones as consciousless self-reflection cuts across this distinction as decisively as "tone" eludes the distinction between the two forms of sensibility, on the one hand, and the difference between sensibility and intelligibility, on the other. The future if not of "philosophy," then of its outcome—projects, that is, which can no longer be seen according to the paradigm of "theory"—announces itself in "tone" to the extent that that "tone," no longer a matter of vision but also no longer simply a matter of invisibility, suspends the hitherto stable distinctions on whose basis theory could come to a conclusion. "Tone," as always, indicates inconclusive commotion.

Not only do the tone of certain incomprehensible sounds and the tone of discourse intended for comprehension share something in common, but this something is itself the axis around which the analogy of speech and art revolves: the division (*Einteilung*) of the arts is projected according to the analogy of the most perfect possible communication (*Mitteilung*). Division and communication, two of the most persistent motifs in the overall orchestration of the third *Critique,* share at the very least a *Teil,* which is not so surprising in a *Kritik der Ur-teils-kraft.* The analogy can take place because the most perfect communication possible is, as Kant notes (*CJ,* 189–90; 5:320), not a matter merely of concepts but also of sensations (*Empfindungen*), and only tone can communicate the latter immediately, without the mediation of concepts, even if its communicability depends on such media as air or ether. The position of tone in the articulation of arts is therefore impossible to reduce; indeed, every reduction of tone—and this henceforth begins to define "tone" in every field of its application—decreases the possibility of communication and makes perfect communication impossible; the very ability to communicate, communicability itself, cannot do without tonality. For this reason, the imperative of tone and the concomitant "dispute" over the proper tone must arise each time the possibility of communication and the ability to communicate are endangered. But *this danger inhabits every tone.* For the tone of discourse and every sensible tone share something in common, and this "something" is not simply the part, not simply the *Teil* judged to be this or that; the shared "part" is also their coming apart, alteration, and *modulation.* As Kant himself asserts (*CJ,* 190; 5:320), modulation, as opposed to articulation and gesture, is the common element in the radically different deployments of "tone." However necessary tone may be for the possibility of communication, it is nevertheless always altering, always modulated, never simply itself; it is, in short, never simple and never pure. Even if every modulation is only implicit, even if it is a mere possibility inherent in its uniformity, modulation underlies the ability of tone to be "itself": to be tonal even when "tone" turns into a *terminus technicus.* Such turning is itself the modulation of the modulation: tone being tonal to the extent that it is no longer "itself." Only by virtue of modulation can there be a uniformity of tone at all, and so modulation is at the very least virtual in so-called pure tones. Alteration of tones, if not a "doctrine" of such alteration, is part of being tonal, part of its ability to communicate and to impart itself in every division of the arts—as modulated, always again altered, always other than itself.

The topic of tone does not simply disturb the divisions and distinctions overseen by the "critical theory" that Kant proposes. Tone is itself the disturbance to the extent that it cannot be itself: not only does it have to change from one domain of application to another, but alteration, as vibration and as modulation, is its very "being": being another, being altered. To modulate means to alter the *modulus;* every *modulus* is already a modulated *modus,* which is itself the "measure" of this modulation. *The measure must modulate:* each of these words in this imperative is itself a modulation of "measure," and together they constitute the imperative of tone. The measure, in other words, must modulate even though there is no measure for the modulation itself. It is, of course, the "musical" measure that first modulates, each measure in music being measured by the specific rhythm or "tact"[25] of the piece. And the rhythm is, once again, the *modus* or the overall measure that constitutes the piece in the first place. But the word *musical* is of little use, since it cannot define "tone" but is, on the contrary, defined by it, as *Tonkunst.* A modicum of tone is necessary in "music" as well as in an indefinite number of other domains because "tone," always altered, is itself this modicum: the measure of the measure, which is itself immense and without measure.

Because of its im-mensity, tone easily becomes "superior,"

claiming to rise beyond every measure while all along only hiding its lack of measure and, to this extent, concealing its own ineluctable emptiness. Tone thus becomes nothing more than the most recent mode of doing things, the measure à la mode. Not only does tone invite fashion (*Mode*), but it is essentially fashionable: no tone is so completely "natural" that it could not be fashioned,[26] and each tone is, in turn, inclined to become the tone of fashion (*Modeton*). Such fashionable tones are indeed the points of departure for both editions of the *Critique of Pure Reason:* whereas the first edition raises its hand against a tone that would discard metaphysics in favor of strictly mechanical sciences, the second edition does battle against the tone that celebrates "genial freedom in thinking" and therefore wants nothing to do with the constraints of rigorous, scientific labor.[27] The change in fashion may not change the *Critique,* but the *Critique* nevertheless changes fashion. For its tone is not that of a *Mode* but—and here is the point of dispute once again—of modernity: it submits all the supposed "knowledge" antiquity has bequeathed to us for our benefit to a thoroughgoing and fundamental critique. Critique thus conquers the field for "the moderns" in this belated battle against those "ancients" who, by translating Plato and invoking his superior, albeit forgotten and incommunicable insights into the nature of all things, fashion a "superior tone." Fashioning themselves as "ancients," Kant's antagonists decry his linguistic and, above all, rhetorical deficiencies,[28] but their ancientness is precisely only a recent mode of speech, only a current fashion of discourse. Fashion and modernity—not precisely the "ancient" and the "modern" but the inversion of this paradigm—thus play out their antagonism in the disputed space of "tone": each one proclaims in its own way the very latest thing, the most recent event, a newly arisen "tone," and makes this proclamation as though it were already enshrined, already "classy" or even, oddly enough, "tony." In ever altering fashion (mode, manner, or *modus*) "tone" reveals itself to be not a fulfilled space but rather a parodic *kairos,* ever emptying itself out, a moment with as little substantial content as permanent form. The modernity of Kant's critique consists in its effort to fashion this empty space into the place of "faith."[29] The fashionableness of his antagonists consists in filling this space with nonmathematical and therefore noncognitive figures.[30] The figure of these figures is, once again, tone "itself": not simply another figure but the one in which each of the expected "visions" or "illuminations" that the figural expression promises is extinguished, as they are all shown to be merely passing, not fulfilling, fads. If fashion, or "tonyness," therefore appears as the truth of "tone," it is because it, modulating without measure, sets into motion the very idea of eternal truth as the commensuration or adequation of representations with something present or ever-present.

Each of these traits of "tone" emerges when Kant ceases to submit the topic of tonality to a theory whose aim is the ascertainment of truth and thus no longer concerns himself with a nontheoretical project that nevertheless understands its debasement from theory as a step away from truth. When Kant judges this topic not according to its truth value but according to its "aesthetic value," its fashionable character becomes unmistakable. The art in which tones are the sole "materials" fashioned into a work—*Tonkunst,* or the art of tones—is judged to be charming, merely emotive, thoroughly empty, always in need of alteration. These traits all converge in its one underlying characteristic: modulation. And modulation is, as it were, a universal language, a language without language, a "metaphorical" language without name, concept, and thus metaphor in the traditional sense. To this extent, sheer modulation is a language without figures, a defigural, nonvisionary, unilluminating, and even light-extinguishing language:

> And just as modulation is, as it were, a universal language of sensations that every human being can understand [*gleichsam eine allegemeine jedem Menschen verständliche Sprache der Empfin-*

> *dung*], so the art of tones [*Tonkunst*] employs this language all by itself in its full force [*in ihrem ganzen Nachdrucke*], namely, as a language of affects; in this way, it universally communicates, according to the law of association, the aesthetic ideas that we naturally connect with such affects. But since these ideas are not concepts, not determinate thoughts, the form of the arrangement of these sensations (harmony and melody), which takes the place of the form of a language, only serves to express [*auszudrücken*], by means of a proportioned attunement [*Stimmung*] of the sensations, the aesthetic idea of a coherent whole of an unnamable fullness of thought [*unnennbaren Gedankenfülle*], and to express it in conformity with a certain theme that is the prevalent affect in the piece. (*CJ*, 198–99; 5:328–29)

The art of tone is a nameless "language"—not a language, properly speaking, but only its unbridled force, the sheer *Nachdruck* (emphasis) of linguistic *Ausdruck* (expression). Nothing is left of language but its emphasis, and yet this emphasis, this *Betonung* as force of impression, is not itself nothing; it is, rather, everything in language that is not nominal, conceptual, predicative, categorial, or even determinate: it is its very power to impress. So indeterminate is this power that it can be understood only according to an empirical law of association, which is as "natural" as the play of tones is "artificial." Nature does not simply emerge here to guarantee an otherwise incomprehensible universal comprehension; nature—and the empirical laws of association—marks the contingency of the communicability that modulation alone can bring to the point of perfection. The languageless language of tone, where "language" as well as "tone" has to be suspended in quotation marks, does not communicate anything; without communicating a "content" or a "form" but replacing both the content of language and the form, it communicates what has hitherto been considered to be "nothing," a nonnatural and nonartificial, unnecessary and nonarbitrary emphatic force, a sheer "toning." *Der Ton betont,* "tone intones": such is the outcome of Kant's exposition of the "aesthetic value," if not the truth, of "tone." And the necessity of this communication of "toning" is bound up with the utter contingency of "association," the naturalness of the connection between affect and aesthetic idea and the artificiality of the "art of tone." An unnamable "language" arises once again, but it arises only as a "language" of feelings, not a real language. Only because it is entirely empty can it suggest a "fullness of thought," and only because it can never amount to more than a "piece" can it impart the idea of a "coherent whole." Arising again and again, this modular "language" can only communicate emphasis rather than content or form; it is therefore always altering between an irksome measure à la mode and a "modernity" that silences all earlier claims to knowledge. Its power to impress has no choice but to express itself as "language," although it is no longer in service of reason. Its impressive power is not exactly positional, not a matter of reason or the I imposing itself; the power is, rather, purely topical, a matter of fashion or modernity.

The topicality of tone—its fashionableness, its modernity, its place within a critical architectonic—derives from its unique ability to dissociate "language" from *logos* and associate it with "laws" that elude, for a time, previous rules of evaluation, even those rules that have hitherto been deemed the only rational ones. Since every tonal association is subject to these laws, every society in which tone plays a part returns, in part, to a "state of nature" and, to this extent, to a potential "state of war." The place of this war is, of course, "tone" itself: at stake is not only *which* tone has been raised and *whether* one has been raised but also precisely what "tone" means. The arbitrariness of all proceedings concerning the status of "tone" cannot be reduced to a law, since no law other than that of tonal association can be used to decide the case, and every such decision is only again topical: another fashion, another mode, another dispute. If "philosophy" is to have a future, it comes in the announcement of a peaceful future: an announcement that is itself always tonal and therefore always hides not exactly some*thing,* neither an unspoken article nor an unwritten clause, but rather "itself," its own modulation at the very least of the word *tone* from the register of "language as it were" to that of language as such. Such modulation implies at the very least a concealment without a corresponding revelation, and thus makes every announcement of an eternal peace in philosophy a piece of "rhetoric": ironic, that is, however much it may wish to present itself as serious and straightforward. Far from lamenting this situation, Kant welcomes it: the treaty for eternal peace is always only nearing; it is always only coming, it never arrives. The future of philosophy therefore lies in the ever modulating modicum, without its own measure, of "tone."

If the future of philosophy is understood as the cessation of all conflict, it will, according to Kant, never arrive, and for good reason. Its arrival would be the death of all thought.[31] If, however, the future of philosophy rests with an *announcement* of "eternal peace," then this future cannot be dissociated from the topic of tone. Each such announcement is unique, and to the extent that it is unique, to the extent that it retreats from generality and universality, it undoes the antagonistic "societies" through which war in philosophy is carried out. And to the extent that such unique announcements are themselves communicated and therefore somehow tonal, they defeat the very purpose of the announcement: to prepare, that is, for the arrival of "eternal peace." Far from dissolving all disputes, these unique announcements of the future foster them—as singular and no longer general disputes. Although it is doubtless tempting to understand the impossibility of philosophy thus reaching its proclaimed future as the deployment of the concept of regulative Ideas to the realm of philosophy (a temptation that is all the more enticing since Kant himself indicates that the *philosopher* is only an "ideal"[32]), such a conception is in error. For the announcement of a final purpose, as an Idea that will henceforth regulate either theoretical or moral activity, not only does not defeat this purpose but in fact promotes it. Quite the opposite is the case with the announcement of a fast approaching treaty for "eternal peace" in philosophy. The announcement is not undertaken under the dictates of a regulative Idea, nor can this announcement be understood as a self-fulfilling prophecy; it is, rather, a counterstatement to all such prophecy insofar as it necessarily defeats the purpose it announces. It disbands the "armies" that have fought on the "battle-field" of metaphysics and thereby turns all disputes into singular ones, "disputes" around which no party can organize except to disband and retreat over again.[33] Kant's retrieval of medical and biological motifs in the "Announcement of a Near Conclusion of a Treaty" doubtless testifies to the irony of treating those who raise a "superior tone" as philosophers at all, but it also indicates his departure from the "ideal" of the philosopher: these unmistakable traits of Kant's "Announcement"—irony, departure from the "ideal," concentration on the function of bodily organs—attest to its ineluctable tonality. Since, moreover, the future of philosophy never arrives, since "eternal peace" can only be announced, every philosophical epoch and, indeed, every text of philosophy will have been traversed by these traits: by, that is, the modicum, modulations, and alterations of tone over which it has lost control. Tracing the effects of tonality is, to this extent, not critical but, for want of a better word, deconstructive.

Such effects are, moreover, not caused but are in their own way original. And no one has shown this more effectively than Kant, for whom the philosophy itself originates in a modulation of tone: a modulation, that is, from the register of sound to that of being itself. Such is the outcome of his archaeological investigation into the origin of philosophy in Pythagoras's exceptional ears. Without being able to make sure of his sources, Kant nevertheless hears with the ears of this other philosopher, who is, not by accident, remembered as the one who began to speak with a philosophical voice:

> But we must not forget *Pythagoras,* about whom, of course, too little is known to have a secure grasp on the metaphysical principles of his philosophy.—Just as Plato awoke to the marvel of *figures* (geometry), so Pythagoras did to that of *numbers* (arithmetic). . . . History says that the discovery of numerical relations *between the tones* and the precise law according to which they alone could be made into music brought him to the following thought: because in this play of sensations mathematics (as the science of numbers) also contains the formal principles of these sensations (and indeed, as it appears, does so a priori, on account of its necessity), an albeit only obscure intuition dwells within us, and this intuition is of a nature that has been ordered according to numerical equivalents by an understanding whose rule extends over nature itself; once applied to the heavenly bodies, this idea can then produce the theory of the harmony of spheres.[34]

At the inception of philosophy is a modulation of "tone" from the register of sound to that of nature in its entirety and therefore to that of being itself. The "tone" of being awoke Pythagoras to speak with the voice of philosophy for the first time, and this already modulated "tone" made it certain that philosophy could never be simply a cognitive exercise expressed in cognitive discourse. Since certain mathematical relations are, as Pythagoras discovered and Kant emphasizes, the *conditio sine qua non* of tones and tonal relations,[35] knowledge (*mathein*), however unconscious,[36] is always somehow implicated in their recognition. Since, however, tones always imply something more than knowledge or less than knowledge; since tone has the power to bring the original philosopher to consciousness—indeed to the self-consciousness of his freedom[37]—and cannot, as a result, be defined in terms of consciousness but, rather, delimits consciousness itself; since "tone" designates, in sum, an unstable dimension in all cognitive discourse; since tones nevertheless have to make themselves known in every discourse, even, and above all, in those that wish to deny their own discursivity and therefore look toward images of awakening into the glories of pure light, the topic of tone cannot help but set philosophy into motion in the first place and keep it in motion, and thus "alive," until the last.

The Ear of the Other is the title of one of Jacques Derrida's many books.[38] But it is also the name of an immense, necessary, and impossible project: to hear with—and along with—the ear of the other. From his earliest remarks on the structure of "hearing-oneself-speak" in Husserl's phenomenology to his reading of Rousseau's theory of the origin of language from the spirit of music, through his overhearing of *glas* ("death knell") in Hegel alongside Genet, and into his "preoccupation" with Hölderlin's doctrine of the alteration of tones, Derrida has made it his task to hear with—and along with—this ear.[39] That the execution of this task entails certain risks is undeniable: they are ones that an altogether secure discourse not only would *not* run but would indeed run away from and erect barriers against. For they are the risks arising from an untenable situation, indeed the site that every secure discourse will not touch: an arena, namely, in which no one can decide who precisely is speaking. Without at least the certainty of this decision, no discourse can secure itself, anchor itself in things and, in turn, tell the truth about anything whatsoever. And no one has made this point better than Kant, for whom the *ego cogito* has no other function than that of serving as the secure identity to which all other identities are referred and therefore in which all recognizable discourse is based. As a result of this function, the difference between inside and outside is assured, and from this firmly established difference the polemic against those who are not philosophers but only pretend to be draws its strength. From the start, the point of such a polemic is to *stop* listening to the other and to hear, once again, oneself: to hear, according to the terms Kant employs, the altogether clear and intimate voice of reason, not that of an enigmatic "oracle."[40]

The other, as the term *oracle* already suggests, can doubtless suffer hypostatization. It (if *it* is the right pronoun) can become the Other: a divine being open only to revelation, or an entity to which all access is denied. Or—and here is the point of the polemic—the other can be understood as the other of oneself: an other who is most itself (if *itself* is the right reflexive pronoun) when it participates in a common ground, a common space, a common sense, or even in the nonempirical and indeed transcendental *sensus communis* presented in the *Critique of Judgment.* To the extent that one can place oneself in the other, one takes part in this communal space and can impart oneself to others.[41] Among the vast array of possible interpretations of otherness and alterity, two stand out and oppose each other with particular virulence; they can even serve to mark the opposition between orthodoxy and Enlightenment: on the one hand, the other whom one is supposed to hear and obey is a "divine" Other; on the other hand, the other to whom one must pay attention and accord respect is the other of myself or, to use Kant's preferred phrase, "humanity in my own person."[42] Kant's polemic against the revival of Neo-Platonism in the guise of sentimental Christianity does indeed present itself as an opposition between these two positions, and it is this opposition that Derrida at once traverses, suspends, and reinscribes. But Derrida conducts this complex operation *along with Kant,* not in opposition to him. For the very point of Kant's polemic—its raising the topic of "tone," its disclosure of the possibility of "eternal peace"—consists in the all-important acknowledgment that no one can decide who is speaking when reason raises its voice: we are unable to say not only whether it is a human or divine voice that makes absolute commands but even whether it is spoken with masculine or feminine intonations: "When we are listening [to this voice of the goddess Isis], we are in doubt whether it comes from man, from the perfected power of his own reason, or whether it comes from an other, whose essence is unknown to us and speaks to man through this, his own reason."[43] Without such an absolutely commanding voice, however, human beings would never be able to know of their freedom, and so the very scientific character of what Kant calls "human philosophy" would promptly collapse—into feelings and sentiments of exaltation.[44] And it is the radical and ineradicable uncertainty concerning the provenance of this voice, the only authentically intimate and inner voice, that underlies the necessity of a "veridical tone": nothing uncertain is to be communicated as though it were certain, including the provenance of the voice that issues the command not to communicate anything uncertain as though it were indeed certain. *A multiplicity of possible voices at the very place where a voice finally speaks with absolute security and complete necessity engenders the future of philosophy as an endless dispute over tone,* and the ineluctable figurality of this "voice" even before it presents itself as that of a goddess guarantees that the disputes over tone will be unable to distinguish themselves from "disputes" over "tone." The overtones of every such "dispute" are clear: there is, namely, a reserve, and therefore an other, that withdraws from every effort at representation as it likewise retreats from every hypostatization. So uncertain is the source of the one voice whose commands are apodictic that it becomes impossible to maintain any longer that this reserve is simply the "humanity in my person" or simply the "divine" other. It (if *it* is the right pronoun) is, rather, the alteration of these others.

No speculation into the provenance of the absolutely commanding voice, as the *dictamen rationis,* will bring it into view: "At bottom we would perhaps do better to rise above and thus spare ourselves research into this matter; since such research is only speculative and since what obliges us (objectively) to act remains always the same, one may place one or the other principle down as a foundation."[45] The vast speculative projects spawned by the *Critiques* knew no other research, and their aim was precisely to overcome the "skeptical" overtones of the statement that the source of all absolutely certain commands is itself uncertain and to secure this source as the conclusion of philosophy in absolute knowledge.[46] Such projects depend on fashioning the other into an object of hearing to which the subject can address inquiries, and only an absolutely hypostatized object—the hypostatic union of subject and object in the divine-human "hypostasis" itself—can guarantee that every such inquiry will find its appropriate answer. To this extent, "speculation" is as foreign to Derrida's project as it is to Kant's. To hear with, and along with, the ear of the other is not to listen *to* the other. It is not to engage in "dialogue," and it is thus not to work out a more inclusive dialectics; it is, above all, not to understand the other as a sender of messages or as an object of address. All of these exercises—listening to the other, obeying the other in oneself, engaging in dialogue and elaborating a dialectics—reduce the ear to an instrument as they exalt, each in its own way, "the other" as an object of hearing. The process of reduction of the ear to a mere instrument could not take the ability to decide with certainty on the figurative function of, for instance, the word *ear* in order to recuperate this function for the purposes of "illustration" or, although this amounts to the same thing, to present it as a mere representation of something that achieves a complete conceptualization at a higher stage. The very openness of the ear, the peculiar structure by virtue of which someone like Pythagoras could suddenly "awaken" to the tone of being itself, is thus relegated to an accident of natural history. Outlining the openness of the ear without the confidence that it is only a figure or an illustration raises the topic of tone precisely because this topic, however immense, again and again eludes those distinctions with which philosophy seeks to bring itself to a close. Each tone implies an ear, and the relation of ear to tone, not that of mind to representations or speaker to something called language, constitutes the locus of Derrida's "critique."

From his earliest readings of Cartesian discourses, Derrida has linked the attempt to bring philosophy to a close with an attempt to stop up the ears in order to hear oneself speak. The closure of philosophy—the exhaustion of its ability to open new ways of determining being, thinking, and knowing—is the subject matter of Derrida's early analyses to the extent that it determines ever more urgent efforts to give philosophy a new and more solid foundation. Opening philosophical activity to efforts other than those of determining the meaning of being, thinking, and knowing has no choice but to sound apocalyptic. And nowhere is this more evident than in those philosophies that, drawing upon Kant's doctrine of "transcendental idealism" and rejecting all "speculation," began to philosophize once again with tones. Since Schopenhauer and the early Nietzsche, each of whom expected a certain revelation from the play of tones, the philosophy of the future has presented itself as a new philosophy of music or as a philosophy of new music. But the "revelation" expected in the art of tone is no longer the one Pythagoras intimated; it is no longer a revelation of the things themselves ordered according to mathematical and therefore fully cognizable functions. The revelation is, rather, understood as that of the utterly irrational Will, and the revelation of this Will at work in music is nothing less than a revelation of the "nullity" of the world.[47] Philosophizing once again with the play of tones raises an apocalyptic tone in which the apocalypse is no longer understood to be, as it was in Pythagoras, a revelation of things themselves but is heard as the cessation of all phenomena: a swallowing up of all things into "the abyss of nothingness" that Schopenhauer for one welcomed as the highest good. The name of the other to whom philosophy is forced to listen if it wants a future at all is no longer God or the humanity in my person but is now the nonhuman, nondivine, strictly irrational Will. But the Will, as Schopenhauer himself emphasizes, is just another name for the essence of the world, and so his metaphysics of the Will cannot escape the closure of philosophy and indeed contributes to its strength. If Schopenhauer discovers a reserve, and therefore an "other," to which representational thought cannot gain access but which certain tonal arrangements can indeed disclose, he immediately abandons this reserve to representational thought by making it into the *opposite* and *essence* of all representations. The apocalyptic tone of this new philosophy of music—and this goes for Nietzsche's philosophy of new music in the *Birth of Tragedy*—arises from its effort to reserve for the purposes of hearing a nondivine and nonhuman other. However much the concept of the Will indicates movement and change, it is nevertheless a hypostatization of the other whose negative determinations—nonhuman, nondivine, unrepresentable, inexplicable, unconscious—all point in the direction of the polemical negation of the Will and therefore of the newly exposed other, the root of all "our" suffering. Every hypostatization of the other into an altogether other ends up in a similar negation and a similar "nihilism." To open philosophy to the ear of the other, which is always "affirmative,"[48] demands an end to the constant attempt to give the hypostatization of the other another name, including the the attempt to call it the Will as manifest in music. The emphasis of every discourse that does not succumb to the closure of philosophy must remain on the ear, not the understanding, of the other and the tone of an apocalypse that is no longer simply revelatory or destructive.

Derrida's most overt examination of the structure of the ear with which philosophy attempts to hear "the other" and to overhear its "exterior" occurs in the preface to *Margins of Philosophy*. As the title of this brief piece, "Tympan," already indicates, the locus of the examination is the indispensable "instrument" that marks the difference between inner and outer ear. Examining the closure of philosophy does not mean piercing this instrument in a vain attempt to open up an unmediated relation to pure exteriority, nor does it mean making this instrument operate more successfully so that it could make the voice of the other clearer and more coherent. It means, rather, examining how the difference between inside and outside has in the course of philosophical discourse organized itself into an organ that philosophy could claim someday to appropriate and thereby to master:

> The *proprius* presupposed in all discourses on economy, sexuality, language, semantics, rhetoric, etc., repercusses its absolute limit only in sonorous representations. Such, at least, is the most insistent hypothesis of this book. A quasi-organizing role is granted, therefore, to the motif of sonic vibration (the Hegelian *Erzittern*) as to the motif of the proximity of the meaning of Being in speech (Heideggerian *Nähe* and *Ereignis*). The logic of the event is examined from the vantage of the structure of expropriation called *timbre* (*tympanum*), *style,* and *signature.* Timbre, style, and signature are the same obliterating division of the proper. They make every event possible, necessary, and unfindable.[49]

Tone is not simply an addition to this list; it is already included in it by virtue of the reference to Hegel,[50] and it can displace and under certain conditions replace each of the others. Showing how tone makes an *apocalyptic* event—the last event, the eventuality of every event—not only possible but also necessary and unfindable is the task undertaken in Derrida's address, and the first step it takes is to show that this event exists nowhere outside its mere announcement: "Come."

Tone solicits an apocalyptic event because, true to the etymology of "solicitation," it makes the whole vibrant.[51] An event has been understood to be apocalyptic as long as it reveals the Other and it destroys everything else; the verification of its announcement, if there is any chance of such verification, has always depended on the survival of a transcendent Other who is the very revealed thing, truth verified in itself. Nothing is so sacred, then, to this understanding of the apocalyptic as the opposition between an occurrence and its announcement. Insofar as "tone," along with timbre, style, and signature, eludes even the most persistent attempts to bring it into line with this opposition, it exposes another "apocalypse": the interruption, namely, of all projects of unveiling and demasking, no matter whether they are undertaken in the name of revealed religion or enlightened discourse. The other announced in an apocalyptic tone (or timbre, style, signature) is not the other with which philosophy has hitherto been concerned:

> Exteriority and alterity are concepts which by themselves have never surprised philosophical discourse. *Philosophy by itself has always been concerned* with them. These are not the conceptual headings under which philosophy's border can be overflowed; the overflow is the object. Instead of determining some other circumscription, recognizing it, practicing it, bringing it to light, forming it, in a word *producing* it (and today this word serves as the crudest "new clothes" of the metaphysical denegation which accommodates itself very well to all these projects), in question will be, but according to a movement unheard of by philosophy, an other which is no longer *its other.*[52]

Such an other is, for instance, the very event of the other, not its occurrence in an ascertainable future but, rather, its eventuality, its *à-venir,* its *Zu-kunft,* its "to-come." The other to come, as an other that never arrives on time or in eternity, cannot present itself as a "divine" Other, as simply "humanity in my person," as the reconciliation of divinity and humanity, or as the irrational Will. On all counts it retreats from such efforts at making it secure, static, hypostatized. To the extent that Derrida's enterprise traces this retreat into the many reserves invented for the purposes of permanent preservation—let it be a thing in itself, the Will, the unconscious, structurality, the unthought, and so forth—the steps of its demonstration parallel the attempts on the part of the "enlightenment" to undo the power of "myth" to enshrine a past world.[53]

To hear with, and along with, the ear of the other is to hear of this event; to hear of it "before" it takes place, of course, because it never does take place. Or its sole venue is in the very solicitation of the event. Since this solicitation, as the placing of the whole into a state of commotion, nevertheless presents itself as an invitation ("Come!"), it soon becomes the object of every critique of the cognitive faculty that does not want to hear of "tone" and therefore does not want to hear with the ear of the other. In this solicitation ("Come!") nothing is revealed, nothing destroyed, but something, which is not a thing properly speaking, is nonetheless concealed: the proper name of the voice speaking, the unique name that guarantees the uniqueness, the authenticity, and even the sincerity of the tone. Every announcement that secures the arrival of the other, on the other hand, reveals something, namely the others with which philosophy has hitherto been concerned: a divine Other, simply "humanity in my person," a hypostatic reconciliation of divine and human, an altogether nondivine and nonhuman Will, or—although this last one must be approached with caution—an event of appropriation, the *Er-eignis* of which Heidegger writes.[54] To hear with, and along with, the ear of the other is to hear the tone of apocalypse: an ever modulating but never moderate tone in which revelation, revelatory speech, and apophantic discourse doubtless takes place but which is itself never a matter of revelation or destruction; it is never itself but is always, if only virtually, another. Without being able to reveal anything, it can nevertheless conceal "itself." Since, however, it conceals "itself" in every announcement, it cannot be made into a thing or a cause over which, say, a decisive dispute could arise. For the very singularity of the solicitation ("Come!") not only cannot preserve itself against repetition but indeed demands it.[55] Once the apocalyptic tone is raised, however, one thing is certain: the other with which philosophy will henceforth be concerned, if one can still speak of "philosophy" here, does not present itself according to the paradigms of previous comprehensibility. If every discourse of unveiling or unmasking, if every attempt to reveal or demonstrate in language can only secure itself by pointing toward a final disclosure "to come," if every discourse is thus a discourse "to come"—not a discourse that can secure itself here and now—and if, in addition, no philosophical discourse can do without the resources drawn from the announcement of its coming to a conclusion, then every one of them is predicated on the uncertifiable "tone" of apocalypse, and so this tone, always altering, proves to be a necessary and, to this extent, "transcendental" condition on philosophical—and not only philosophical—discourse. Such at least is the hypothesis Derrida "submits to discussion"[56] and thus opens for dispute.

Notes

1. Johann Schlosser, Kant's principal antagonist, died in 1798, soon after completing his rejoinder to Kant's "Announcement of the Near Conclusion of a Treaty for Eternal Peace in Philosophy." Count Friedrich Leopold zu Stolberg, an antagonist whom Kant does not mention by name, converted to Catholicism in 1800. Schlosser and Stolberg, as well as the general controversy stirred by Kant's polemics against them, are discussed in detail in the notes to the translations of Kant's essays below.

2. See Immanuel Kant, *Critique of Pure Reason,* trans. Norman Kemp Smith (New York: St. Martin's Press, 1965), 8; A viii.

3. See, in particular, the second appendix to the "Eternal Peace: A Philosophical Sketch" (1795). The transcendental formula of public right is "all actions that affect the rights of other men are wrong if their maxim is not consistent with publicity" (Immanuel Kant, *Perpetual Peace and Other Essays,* trans. Ted Humphrey [Indianapolis, Ind.: Hackett Publishing Co., 1983], 135; 8:181).

4. See the final remarks of the "Announcement of the Near Conclusion of a Treaty for Eternal Peace in Philosophy," 93 below.

5. On the complex etymology of *Ton* in German, see the vertiginous compilation of Jacob and Wilhelm Grimm, *Deutsches Wörterbuch,* ed. M. Lexer and D. Krakik (Leipzig: Hirzel, 1935), XI.1: 681–751 and beyond (for the various compounds made from the word). The German word *Ton* apparently has two sources, one Greco-Latin, the other Germanic. The word in Latinate languages generally refers back to the Greek *tonos* (cords, including vocal ones, that are "strained" to the point where they make distinctly different kinds of sound), and it was perhaps further influenced by the Latin *tonare* ("to thunder"). The word *Ton* in German—and

perhaps in English equivalent—is also related to the Old German *duna, dynian* ("to make noise"); its modern English equivalent is "din." Since *dynian* could designate the "quaking" and "droning" (*Beben* and *Dröhnen*) of the earth, it too was related to large-scale vibrational strains; earthquakes made noise as they released underground tensions. "Early on *don* as 'din' and 'noise' must have touched upon and crossed with *dôn* as 'melody'" (Grimm and Grimm, *Deutsches Wörterbuch,* XI.1: 684).

By the middle of the eighteenth century, *tone* had, according to the Grimm brothers, become a fashionable word first in France and then in Germany; indeed, it became a word for the fashion of discourse, *Modeton.* The compilation of citations the Grimm brothers amass easily supports this contention. (It is remarkable that the Grimm brothers do not cite Kant but not at all so that they seem to know nothing of Hölderlin's "doctrine" of the alteration of tones.) The word became fashionable—and a word for "fashion"—during a time in which sentiments and feelings (*Stimmungen* in the widest sense) were given the task of restraining the universal claims of an "enlightened" reason. No word could be more appropriate to counter the starkly visual character and culture of the *Aufklärung,* but it likewise offered itself as a means for the development of a more or less "scientific" manner of classifying social types (see, for example, Adolf Knigge, *Ueber den Umgang mit Menschen* [1788; reprint, Essen: Phaidon, 1991]).

6. See the conclusion to Kant, *Allgemeine Naturgeschichte und Theorie des Himmels, Kants Gesammelte Schriften,* ed. Königliche Preussische [later, Deutsche] Akademie der Wissenschaften (Berlin and Leipzig: Walter de Gruyter, 1902–), 1:367; trans. as *Universal Natural History and Theory of the Heavens,* trans. Stanley L. Jaki (Edinburgh: Scottish Academic Press, 1981), 196. All further quotations of Kant refer to the Akademie edition except in the case of the *Critique of Pure Reason,* where reference is made to the A and B editions. On this passage, cf. Peter Fenves, *A Peculiar Fate: Metaphysics and World-History in Kant* (Ithaca, N.Y.: Cornell University Press, 1991), 80–82.

7. See Kant, *Universal Natural History,* 161; 1:322.

8. See the account of "the noble sublime" in Kant's *Observations on the Feelings of the Beautiful and the Sublime,* trans. J. T. Goldthwait (Berkeley: University of California Press, 1965), 48–49; 2:209–10.

9. An attempt to redescribe Kantian thought as a field of incommensurable discourses whose various "transitions" are all unjust—but nonetheless necessary—negotiations undertaken under the de-

mand of justice has been pursued for many years in the work of Jean-Francois Lyotard; see, for instance, Lyotard, *L'Enthusiasme: La Critique kantienne de l'histoire* (Paris: Editions Galilée, 1986); cf. Lyotard, *The Differend: Phrases in Dispute,* trans. Georges Van Den Abbeele (Minneapolis: University of Minnesota Press, 1988). On Kant's "style," his concept of *Darstellung* (presentation, exposition), and their relation to the question of tone, see Jean-Luc Nancy, *Le Discours de la syncope* (Paris: Aubier-Flammarion, 1976), esp. 82–91. For an amplification of Lyotard's and Nancy's work in the context of the question concerning the "future of thought," see Francoise Proust, *Kant, le ton de l'histoire* (Paris: Editions Payot, 1991).

10. See Kant's description of the "bloodless battles" in the shadow world of "Valhalla" (A 756; B 785) and the shadow-ridden "sea" of illusion (A 236; B 295). On the possibility of developing a fundamental metaphorics on the basis of certain Kantian conceptions of sensibility, see Jacques Derrida, "The White Mythology," *Margins of Philosophy,* trans. Alan Bass (Chicago: University of Chicago Press, 1982), 227–29.

11. See 87 below.

12. For Hölderlin's doctrine of the alteration of tones (*Wechsel der Töne*) see, above all, "On the Difference of Poetic Modes," *Sämtliche Werke,* ed. Friedrich Beissner (Stuttgart: Kohlhammer, 1943–85), 6:266–72; Hölderlin, *Essays and Letters on Theory,* trans. Thomas Pfau (Albany: State University of New York Press, 1988). Cf. Lawrence Ryan, *Hölderlins Lehre vom Wechsel der Töne* (Stuttgart: Kohlhammer, 1960).

13. Cf. *Critique of Pure Reason* (A 745; B 777).

14. See Kant, *The Conflict of the Faculties,* intro. Mary J. Gregor, trans. Mary J. Gregor and Robert E. E. Anchor (New York: Abaris, 1979), 33; 7:55; cf. 41; 7:71.

15. See below, 56.

16. See below, 93.

17. On Kant and lying, see my essay "Testing Right—Lying in View of Justice," *Cardozo Law Review* 13:4 (December 1991): 1081–1113.

18. See below, "On a Newly Arisen Superior Tone in Philosophy" (56–57) and the discussion above, 29.

19. See Kant, *Critique of Judgment,* trans. Werner S. Pluhar (Indianapolis, Ind.: Hackett Publishing Co., 1987), 198; 5:327. Hereafter, this work will be cited as *CJ* in the text.

20. See the influential volume edited by Karl-Otto Apel, *Sprachpragmatik und Philosophie* (Frankfurt am Main: Suhrkamp, 1982).

21. See Kant, *Prolegomena to Any Future Metaphysics,* trans. Paul Carus and James W. Ellington (Indianapolis, Ind.: Hackett Publishing Co., 1977), 115; 4:375.

22. The vacillations and hesitations of this elucidation have already been analyzed with exemplary rigor by Derrida in the opening paragraphs of "Parergon," *The Truth in Painting,* trans. Geoff Bennington and Ian McLeod (Chicago: University of Chicago Press, 1987), 52–82.

23. See the final paragraphs in the final section on "beauty as the symbol of morality" (*CJ,* 227–28; 5:352–53). On the deployment of "analogy" in the *Critique of Judgment* in general, see Jacques Derrida, "Economimesis," trans. Richard Klein, *Diacritics* 11:2 (Summer 1981): 3–25.

24. The paragraph (§ 51) concludes with an extraordinary show of indecisiveness and inconclusiveness, and not even Werner Pluhar's extensive and incisive note (*CJ,* 195) can sufficiently sort out the aporia in which Kant finds himself and loses his "theory" of aesthetics. For the entire theoretical status of the critique of taste is indeed at stake. If this critique adjudicates taste on the basis of a theorem concerning the operation of the mind, it cannot reveal the "harmonious" interaction of the cognitive faculties in every judgment that something is beautiful. Kant continued his reflections on this matter in an exchange of letters with Christoph Friedrich Hellwag (see 11:232–34) and pursued the matter of the "ether" into his very last work, the *opus postumum.* In an unpublished essay on the relation of the third *Critique* and the *opus postumum,* Eckart Förster has shown how Kant's renewed interest in the problem of the ether may very well have influenced an alteration in § 14 that makes color into the exact analogue of tone.

25. See below, 62.

26. In § 42 of the *Critique of Judgment* on the "intellectual interest in the beautiful," Kant shows how in the case of tone the "as it were, language that speaks to us and which seems to have a higher meaning" can be artificially produced; once the artifice is detected, the "higher meaning" reveals itself to be a "base" intention: to make money (*CJ,* 169; 5:302).

27. According to the preface of the first edition of the *Critique of Pure Reason* (1781), the "fashionable tone" (*Modeton*) so despises metaphysics that she (*die Metaphysik*) becomes a "matron outcast and forsaken, she mourns like Hecuba" (A xiii; cf. Fenves, *Peculiar Fate,* 7–8). By the time of the second edition (1787), the "fashionable tone" had altered, but it promises to alter in turn: "I have

perceived, with pleasure and thankfulness, in various published works . . . that the spirit of thoroughness has not died out but has only been drowned out for a short time by the fashionable tone of a genial freedom in thinking [*durch den Modeton einer geniemäßigen Freiheit im Denken auf kurze Zeit überschrien worden*]" (B xlii–xliii). The *Critiques* suspend these two extremes of tone, each of which is fashionable for a time, in order to prepare the way for another, unnamed tone, which will be just as fashionable as the others.

28. See below, 91.

29. See the famous lines in the preface to the second edition of the *Critique of Pure Reason*, B xxx.

30. See below, 64.

31. See below, 87.

32. See the *Critique of Pure Reason* (A 838–39; B 866–67). Up until the *Critique*, philosophy was "a merely scholastic concept—a concept of a system of knowledge which is sought solely in its character as a science." As a result of the *Critique*, it becomes a world-concept: "the science of the relation of all knowledge to the essential ends of human reason." Similar remarks are to be found in the *opus postumum* (see, for instance, 21:40).

33. On the structure of the self-fulfilling prophecy and its significance for Kant's last writings on history and politics, see Margherita von Brentano, "Kants Theorie der Geschichte und der bürgerlichen Gesellschaft" in *Spiegel und Gleichnis*, ed. N. W. Bolz and W. Hübener (Würzburg: Königshausen and Neumann, 1983), 205–14; cf. Fenves, *Peculiar Fate*, 184–88.

34. See below, 54–55; last italics added.

35. See, for instance, *CJ*, 199; 5:329.

36. According to Leibniz, music was only an unconscious counting; see, for instance, the famous § 17 of his "Principles of Nature and Grace, Based on Reason" (1714): "Music charms us, although its beauty consists only in the agreement of numbers and in the counting, which we do not perceive but which the soul nevertheless continues to carry out, of the beats of vibrations of the sounding bodies which coincide at certain intervals" (Gottfried Wilhelm von Leibniz, *Philosophical Papers*, ed. Leroy E. Loemker [Dordrecht, Holland: Reidel, 1976], 641). A philosophy of music reverberates through Leibniz's work from his principle of "pre-established harmony" to his reinterpretation of the doctrine of the music of spheres and his argument for the aesthetic necessity of dissonance (physical and moral evil).

37. See below, 55. As Kant develops this reading of the origin of

philosophy in Pythagoras's extraordinary ears, he comes across the intimation of "freedom" in the doctrine of musical modes. That Kant cannot make sure of his sources is due in no small measure to the "silence" Pythagoras imposed on his band of philosophical followers. For an energetic description of the Pythagorean cult, see Kant's presentation of the history of philosophy in the *Logic:* "*When* and *where* among the Greeks the philosophical spirit first sprang up—this cannot be determined. . . . Around the time of the Ionian school there arose in Greece a man of rare genius, who not only established a school but at the same time designed and carried out a project the like of which had never been before. This was Pythagoras, born of the isle of Samos. He founded a society of philosophers who were united in a league by the law of secrecy [*Verschwiegenheit*]. . . . The object of his league seems to have been none other than *to purify religion from the delusions of the people, to moderate tyranny, and to introduce greater legality into the states*" (Kant, *Logic,* trans. and intro. R. S. Hartman and W. Schwarz [Indianapolis: Bobbs-Merrill, 1974], 32–33; 9:28–29). This presentation of Pythagoras, which is certainly the most detailed and lively one of any philosopher in his "Short Outline of a History of Philosophy," makes him, on the one hand, into an authentic forerunner of Kant for whom the purification of religion and the institution of a lawful constitution were inseparable from an ethic of universal communicability, and, on the other hand, into a forerunner of "superior" philosophers—or at least of "lodge members" claiming to be philosophers (see below 51)—who depend on secrecy to secure their identity and community.

38. See Jacques Derrida, *The Ear of the Other: Otobiography, Transference, Translation,* ed. Christie V. McDonald, trans. Peggy Kamuf and Avital Ronell (New York: Schocken, 1985).

39. For these motifs, see Jacques Derrida, *Speech and Phenomenon,* trans. David Allison (Evanston, Ill.: Northwestern University Press, 1979); Derrida, *Of Grammatology,* trans. Gayatri Spivak (Baltimore: Johns Hopkins University Press, 1976), 314–15; Derrida, *Glas,* trans. John P. Leavey, Jr., and Richard Rand (Lincoln: University of Nebraska Press, 1986); Derrida, *The Post Card: From Socrates to Freud and Beyond,* trans. Alan Bass (Chicago: University of Chicago Press, 1987), esp. 202. Comments on certain of Derrida's previous considerations of tonality can be found in the discussion that followed his presentation of "On a Newly Arisen Apocalyptic Tone in Philosophy" at the conference "departing " from his work and, above all, from the essay in his *Margins of Philosophy* called

"The Ends of Man." See Philippe Lacoue-Labarthe and Jean-Luc Nancy, eds., *Les Fins de l'homme. A partir du travail de Jacques Derrida* (Paris: Galilée, 1981), 480–86.

40. See below, 52.

41. See § 40 of the *Critique of Judgment,* "On Taste as a Kind of *Sensus Communis*" (*CJ,* 149–62; 5:293–96). As is well known, Hans-Georg Gadamer begins *Truth and Method* with a long discussion of the history and heritage of this concept in order to show how "the other" is indeed the partner of a conversation; see H.-G. Gadamer, *Truth and Method,* trans. J. Weinsheimer and D. G. Marshall (New York: Crossroads, 1989), 19–34; see also the discussion of Gadamer's work in relation to Derrida in D. P. Michelfelder and R. E. Palmer, eds., *Dialogue and Deconstruction* (Albany: State University of New York Press, 1989).

42. This phrase gains particular weight for Kant in his last writings on ethics; see, for instance, the important footnote in the introduction to the second section of the *Metaphysics of Morals,* trans. as *The Doctrine of Virtue,* trans. and intro. Mary J. Gregor (Philadelphia: University of Pennsylvania Press, 1964), 37; 6:379.

43. See below, 71.

44. To draw on the concepts Kant first developed in *Foundations for the Metaphysics of Morals* (1784), moral commands are the *ratio cognoscendi* of freedom, whereas freedom is the *ratio essendi* of moral obligation (see Kant, *Foundations of the Metaphysics of Morals,* trans. and intro. Lewis White Beck [Indianapolis, Ind.: Bobbs-Merrill, 1959], 72–74; 4:453–56).

45. See below, 71.

46. On the relation of Kant's presentation of Isis and the development of Hegelian dialectics, see Derrida, *Glas;* cf. Werner Hamacher, "*pleroma*—zu Genesis und Struktur einer dialektischen Hermeneutik bei Hegel," in *Der Geist des Christentums,* ed. W. Hamacher (Frankfurt am Main: Ullstein, 1987), esp. 97–105.

47. See Arthur Schopenhauer, *The World as Will and Representation,* trans. E. F. J. Payne (New York: Dover, 1958), 1:255–67; 2:447–57; cf. Schopenhauer, *Essays and Aphorisms,* trans. R. J. Hollingdale (Penguin: Harmondsworth, England, 1970), 155–65. Music is, for Schopenhauer, the "copy of the will itself" (*World as Will and Representation,* 1:257); indeed, "music expresses in an exceedingly universal language, in a homogeneous material, that is, in mere tones, and with the greatest distinctness and truth, the inner being, the in-itself, of the world, which we think of under the concept of the will" (264). Proof of the irrationality of the will can even

be found in the irrationality of the numerical relations of certain harmonies: "The numbers themselves, by which the tones can be expressed, have insoluble irrationalities" (266). And tones are "irrational" in the sense that they do not call out for a reason or cause: "For tones make the aesthetic impression as effect, and this without going back to their causes, as in the case of perception" (266). In contrast to Schopenhauer's unproblematic assurance that the Will reveals itself in music, Nietzsche makes its revelation—or, as he says, its "appearance"—into an immense problem, indeed, the one from which *The Birth of Tragedy* departs and the one on which perhaps all of Nietzsche's later writings converge; see Nietzsche, *The Birth of Tragedy,* trans. Walter Kaufmann (New York: Vintage, 1967), esp. 44–50. One later student of Schopenhauer must be cited in this context, namely Ludwig Wittgenstein. If, as Wittgenstein asserts, "it is impossible to speak about the will in so far as it is the subject of ethical [and therefore aesthetic] attributes" (*Tractatus Logico-Philosophicus,* trans. D. F. Pears and B. F. McGuinness [London: Routledge and Kegan Paul, 1961], 147), this impossibility does not imply that the Will, no longer understood as a psychological phenomenon, cannot show itself otherwise, specifically in certain genial arrangements of tones. As many readers of the *Tractatus* have understood, the necessarily implicit counterpart to "language" is music. (For Wittgenstein's later remarks on the relation of music to language and his reference to Schopenhauer's presentation, see Ludwig Wittgenstein, *Culture and Value,* ed. G. H. von Wright, trans. Peter Winch [Chicago: University of Chicago Press, 1984], esp. 34.)

48. See Derrida's announcement of a new, "affirmative" phase in the project of deconstructive interpretation, *Spurs: Nietzsche's Styles / Eperons: Les Styles de Nietzsche,* trans. Barbara Harlow (Chicago: University of Chicago Press, 1979), 36.

49. Derrida, *Margins of Philosophy,* xix.

50. For Derrida's analysis of the function of *Ton* in Hegel, see *Margins of Philosophy,* 92–95.

51. On *solicit,* see the paragraphs that close the essay "The Ends of Man": "Is not this security of the near what is trembling today, that is, the co-belonging and co-propriety of the name of man and the name of Being. . . . But this trembling—which can only come from a certain outside—was already requisite within the very structure it solicits" (Derrida, *Margins of Philosophy,* 133; as Alan Bass has repeatedly emphasized, *solicit* derives from *sollus* and *ciere,* to set "the whole" into a resonating "motion").

52. Derrida, *Margins of Philosophy,* xiii–xiv.

53. Each of the issues raised in this context—myth, enlightenment, tonality—has been scrutinized again and again by Theodor Adorno. His *Philosophy of Modern* [*New*] *Music,* which serves as an excursus to his and Max Horkheimer's *Dialectic of Enlightenment,* orients its analysis of the difference between progressive and regressive modes of new music according to one criterion: whether it contributes to the reification of the other or whether it liquidates this process of reification. Twelve-tone and atonal composition resist the regressive and "mythic" impulses toward uniformity that arise from the specific relations of modern production; see Adorno, *Philosophy of Modern Music,* trans. G. Mitchell and W. V. Blomster (New York: Seabury, 1973). But Adorno's most instructive, if not altogether transparent, consideration of the topic of tone can be found in *The Jargon of Authenticity,* his polemic against Heidegger. This hasty polemic, which is also an excursus to the *Dialectic of Enlightenment,* can easily be seen as a revision of Kant's "On a Newly Arisen Superior Tone in Philosophy." It attacks Heidegger and the "authentics" for their haughty tone, their stately emphasis (*Betonung*), and their tonal mode (*Tonart*): "What is or is not the jargon is determined by whether the word is written in an intonation which places it transcendentally in opposition to its own meaning" (Theodor Adorno, *The Jargon of Authenticity,* trans. Knut Tarnowski and Frederic Will [Evanston, Ill.: Northwestern University Press, 1973], 8). Speaking "the jargon" is, translated into Kant's terms, "acting the philosopher." And everyone who speaks in the jargon takes on an apocalyptic tone: "The tone of the jargon has something in it of the seriousness of the augurs. . . . The fact that the words of the jargon sound as if they said something higher than what they mean suggests the term 'aura'" (9). Adorno goes so far as to conclude with a critique of Heidegger's "tone of voice" (164) by way of Schiller's "On Grace and Dignity," a text that Kant subjected to the same treatment applied to the texts of those who wrote in a "superior tone" (see below, 112–13).

54. Each motif in the thematics of tone can be reassembled around the thought of *Ereignis;* indeed, an alteration of tone, or modulation of the tonal mode (*Tonart*), exposes the "critical zone" of its arrival. Or, at least, such is the point of *Der Satz vom Grund* ("the principle of reason," or "the leap from the ground"). The principle of reason ("nothing is without a reason, cause, or ground") leads to the "critical zone" in which critique itself stands or falls on the question of emphasis (*Betonung*): either the "is" or

the "nothing" is intoned. Hearing the difference between these two intonations decides the fate—or "sending"—of being (see Martin Heidegger, *Der Satz vom Grund* [Pfullingen: Neske, 1957], esp. 84–92). Only by hearing another tonal mode, which is perhaps the tonal mode of the other, can the *Ereignis* be announced. Yet this hearing, Heidegger emphasizes, is not *with* the ear; it has nothing to do with instruments or organs (87). This categorical exclusion of the ear as an instrument, like so many uncritical discussions of hearing, easily captures its point by the hackneyed example of Beethoven, who wrote music while deaf. And this exclusion, which Derrida scrupulously avoids, lets Heidegger declare that the hearing of which he speaks, including the hearing of another tonal mode in the principle of reason, is absolutely not "metaphorical," since metaphor pertains only to metaphysics (89). For Derrida's analysis of this passage in which the terms of the retreat from metaphor and metaphysics are examined, see his "*Retrait* of Metaphor," trans. F. Gasdner et al., *Enclitic* 2 (1978): 5–33.

55. In the discussion that followed the delivery of "On a Newly Arisen Apocalyptic Tone in Philosophy," Derrida makes a remark from which one could present an idea of tragedy no less powerful than those of Nietzsche and Walter Benjamin: "A mimesis opens the fiction of tone. It is the tragedy of 'Come' that it must be repeatable (*a priori* repeated in itself) in order to resonate" (*Les Fins de l'homme,* 480).

56. See below, 156.

Kant

On a Newly Arisen Superior Tone in Philosophy

* * *

[8:389] Since it relinquished its first meaning, scientific wisdom of life [*wissenschaftliche Lebensweisheit*], the name of philosophy has very early on come into demand as a title that would adorn the minds of uncommon thinkers who now imagine it to be a mode whereby secrets are revealed.—To the *ascetics* in the Marcarian desert, philosophy meant their *monasticism.* The *alchemist* called himself *philosophus per ignem.*[1] Tradition has made the *Masons* of ancient and modern times adepts of a secret about which they jealously *want* to say nothing (*philosophus per initiationem*). The newest owners of this secret are, finally, those who have it *in themselves* but unfortunately *cannot* express and universally communicate it through language (*philosophus per inspirationem*). If there were knowledge of the supersensible (from a theoretical point of view, this alone is a true secret) that is indeed possible to reveal to human understanding from a practical point of view, such knowledge drawn from the understanding, as the faculty of knowledge by means of *concepts,* would nevertheless be far inferior to the knowledge that, as a faculty of *intuition,* could be immediately perceived by the understanding. For, by means of the first procedure, the discursive understanding must expend a great amount of labor to analyze its concepts and then arrange them according to principles, and it must climb many difficult steps in order to make progress in knowledge; instead of this labor, an *intellectual intuition* would immediately present the object and grasp it all at once. Whoever believes himself to be in possession of intellectual intuition will look down on the former procedure with contempt; and, conversely, the very ease of such an employment of reason is a powerful lure to boldly assume a faculty of intellectual intuition and likewise to recommend that philosophy is best founded on it. This can easily be explained from a natural propensity of human beings toward selfishness, which reason observes in silence.

[390] It lies not merely in the natural laziness but also in the vanity of human beings (a misunderstood freedom) that those who *have a living,* whether it be a wealthy or a poor one, consider themselves *superior* [*Vornehme*] in comparison to those who must work.—The *Arab,* or *Mongol,* has contempt for city dwellers and considers himself superior in comparison with them, for driving around in the desert with his horses and sheep is more entertaining than work. A member of the forest people of *Tunguses* intends to throw a curse at his brother when he says: "May you rear your own cattle like a *Burait*!" The brother hurls back this malediction by saying: "May you work in the fields like the *Russian*!" The latter will perhaps, according to his way of thought, give the response: "May you sit at the weaver's loom like the German!"—In a word: all think themselves superior to the degree that they believe themselves exempt from work; and, following this principle, matters have recently gone so far that a purported philosophy announces itself openly and without an effort at concealment; in this philosophy one need not *work* but only listen to and enjoy the oracle within oneself in order to bring all the wisdom envisioned with philosophy into one's possession: and this announcement is indeed made in a tone indicating that the superior ones do not think of themselves in the same class as those who, in a scholarly manner, consider themselves obligated to progress slowly and carefully from the critique of their faculty of knowledge to dogmatic knowledge.[2] Rather, they are, like geniuses, already in a position to achieve everything that hard work alone can bring and indeed to achieve more than that by a single penetrating glance into their interior. No doubt some people can in a pedantic way be *proud* of sci-

ences that demand work, like mathematics, natural science, ancient history, philology, and so forth, even proud of philosophy insofar as it is necessarily involved with the methodical development and systematic arrangement of concepts. Yet no one but the philosopher of *intuition,* who does not demonstrate his power through the Heraculean labor of self-knowledge, which goes from the bottom up, but shows his power, as he flies above all labor, through an apotheosis that comes from above and that costs him nothing—no one but this philosopher can come up with the notion of acting *superior,* because, being up there, he speaks from his own viewpoint, and so he is not bound to speak with anyone.

And now to the things themselves!

---

[391] *Plato,* who was as good a mathematician as a philosopher, admired in the properties of certain geometric figures, e.g., the circle, a kind of purposiveness, that is, a fitness to solve a manifold of problems, or a manifold of solutions to one and the same problem (as in the theory of geometric loci) starting from a single principle; it is as if the demand for the construction of certain concepts of size were *intentionally* planted in them, although one could a priori perceive and prove them to be necessary. But purposiveness can be conceived as a cause only by relating the object to an understanding.

Since we, with our understanding, as a faculty of knowledge through *concepts,* cannot a priori extend knowledge beyond our concepts (an extension that does nevertheless actually take place in mathematics), Plato had to assume that we human beings had a priori intuitions that did not have their first *origin* in *our* understanding (for our understanding is a discursive faculty and thus a faculty of thought, not of intuition) but rather in the kind of understanding that is at the same time the originary basis of all things: a divine understanding whose intuitions are *direct* and thus deserve to be called archetypes (Ideas). But our intuition of these divine *Ideas* (for we must have had an intuition a priori, if we wished to make comprehensible to ourselves the capacity to have synthetic propositions a priori in pure mathematics) are imparted to us only *indirectly,* as imitations (ectypa)—to use an image, as shadow-images of all things that we know a priori by way of synthesis. But our birth has led to the obscuring of these Ideas by making us forget their origin; consequently, our mind (here called the soul) has been trapped in a body whose fetters it must now be the noble job of philosophy gradually to loosen.[1]

[392] But we must not forget *Pythagoras,* about whom, of course, too little is known to have a secure grasp on the metaphysical principles of his philosophy.—Just as Plato awoke to the marvel of *figures* (geometry), so Pythagoras did

[1] At least Plato proceeded in a consistent manner throughout all these conclusions. There is no doubt that a question hovered before his mind, although in an obscure manner, and this question has only recently been clearly articulated: "How are synthetic propositions a priori possible?" If he had then been able to come up with what was discovered only much later: namely, that there are indeed intuitions a priori, although they do not belong to human understanding but are rather *sensible* (with the titles space and time); that we therefore know all objects of the senses merely as appearances, and even their forms, which we can determine a priori in mathematics, are not those of things in themselves but rather (subjective) forms of our sensibility, [392] which are therefore valid for all objects of possible experience but not anything beyond that—if Plato had only come up with this solution, he would not have sought pure intuitions (which he needed in order to make comprehensible synthetic knowledge a priori) in the divine understanding and its archetypes of all things, as independent objects, and so he would not have kindled the torch of exaltation.—For he certainly perceived this much: if he wished to be able to assert that he intuited *empirically* the object in itself in the intuition that lies at the basis of geometry, geometric judgment and all of mathematics would be merely a science founded on experience, which would contradict the *necessity* that (along with its intuitiveness) is precisely what secures it such a high rank among all the sciences.

to that of *numbers* (arithmetic); that is, his attention was attracted to the appearance of a certain purposiveness and an, as it were, intentionally implanted fitness in the character of numbers to solve numerous rational tasks of mathematics, where intuition a priori (space and time) and not merely discursive thought must be presupposed; he assumed a kind of *magic* simply in order to make comprehensible the possibility of extending not only our concepts of quantity in general but also their particular and, as it were, secret properties.—History says that the discovery of numerical relations between the tones and the precise law according to which they alone could be made into music brought him to the following thought: because in this play of sensations mathematics (as the science of numbers) also contains the formal principles of these sensations (and indeed, as it appears, does so a priori, on account of its necessity), an albeit only obscure intuition dwells within us, and this intuition is of a nature that has been ordered according to numerical equivalents by an understanding whose rule extends over nature itself; once applied to the heavenly bodies, this idea can then produce the theory of the harmony of the spheres. Now, nothing is more enlivening to the senses than music; the enlivening principle in man is, however, the *soul;* and since music, according to Pythagoras, merely rests on perceived numerical relations and (something to note well) the enlivening principle in a human being—the soul—is at the same time a free, self-determining being, his definition of the soul—*anima est numerus se ipsum movens* [the soul is a number that moves itself]—can perhaps be understood and to a certain extent even justified, if one assumes [393] that the capacity to move on one's own was supposed to indicate the difference between the soul and matter, which in itself is lifeless and can be moved only by something exterior, and so this capacity was supposed to indicate freedom.

It was therefore *mathematics* about which Pythagoras as well as Plato *philosophized* when they considered all knowledge a priori (it could contain intuitions or concepts) intellectual, and they believed that this philosophy had come upon a *secret* where there was no secret: not because reason can answer all the questions with which it is concerned but because the oracle of reason is struck dumb if a question has been raised so high that it no longer makes any sense. If, for example, geometry proposes several properties of the circle that are called *beautiful* (as one can find in Montucla)[3] and if now the question is raised—"From where does this circle get these properties, which seem to contain a kind of extensive usefulness and purposiveness?"—then no other answer can be given but this one: *Quaerit delirus quod non respondet Homerus* [A fool asks what Homer cannot answer]. Whoever wishes to solve a mathematical problem philosophically contradicts himself; for example, Why is it that the *rational* relationship of three sides of a right-angled triangle can be none other than that of the numbers 3, 4, 5?[4] But the one who *philosophizes* beyond a mathematical problem believes that he has hit upon a secret and even believes he sees something extravagantly great where he sees nothing; and he posits true philosophy (*philosophia arcani*) in precisely the fact that he broods over an Idea in himself, which he can neither make comprehensible nor even communicate to others, and so here poetic talent finds nourishment for itself in the feelings and enjoyment of exalting [*im Gefühl und Genuß zu schwärmen*]: which is, to be sure, far more inviting and splendid than the law of reason whereby one must work to acquire a possession. But here also poverty and haughtiness yield the most ridiculous phenomenon: hearing philosophy spoken in a *superior tone*.

The philosophy of *Aristotle* is, in contrast, work. But I will consider him here only (as in the two previous cases) as a metaphysician, that is, as one who analyzes all knowledge a priori into its elements, and as an artisan of reason who puts these elements back together from reason (from the categories); his work, as far as it reached, had its usefulness, although it did indeed meet up with misfortune as it *pro-*

gressed, since he extended the same principles that are valid for sensibility to the supersensible (without noticing the dangerous leap he was then forced to make), and these principles were so far extended that his categories no longer [394] applied. It was necessary at that point to divide and measure beforehand the organ of thinking in itself—namely, reason—according to its own fields, the theoretical and the practical, but such work was reserved for later times.

Now we want to hear and appreciate the new tone of philosophizing (in which one can do without philosophy).

That *superior* persons [ones from the noble class] philosophize, even if this superiority were to elevate them to the heights of metaphysics, must be counted among their greatest honors, and their (hardly avoidable) mistakes against the School deserve indulgence, since they condescend to put themselves in the same shoes of civic equality.[2] That, how-

[2]There is indeed a difference between philosophizing and acting the philosopher.[a] The latter takes place in a superior tone, if despotism over the reason of the people (indeed over one's own reason) achieved by shackling the people to a blind faith passes for philosophy. Such is the case, for example, in the "faith in the thunder-legion at the time of Marcus Aurelius" as well as the faith "in the fire ignited by a miracle from the ruins of Jerusalem that smote Julian the Apostate."[b] This passes for authentic, genuine philosophy, and its opposite is called "blind disbelief" [*Köhlerunglaube,* faithlessness of the coal burner] (exactly as if the coal burners, deep in their woods, were notorious for being faithless, considering the fairy tales told about them); in addition to this, there is the assurance that philosophy came to an end two thousand years ago, because "the Stagirite has conquered so much for science that he has left behind little of importance for his followers to espy."[c] Likewise, there are not only egalitarians of the political constitution who, in accordance with Rousseau, want all citizens of a State to be

ever, would-be philosophers act *superior* can in no way warrant any indulgence, since they lift themselves above *their comrades in the guild* and injure their inalienable right to freedom and equality in matters of reason alone.

[395] The principle of wanting to philosophize under the influence of a higher *feeling* is, among all principles, the one best suited to produce a superior tone. For who will contest my own feelings? If I can make it credible that this feeling is not merely subjective *in me* but can be demanded of everyone and is therefore held to be objectively valid and rationalized as a piece of knowledge, therefore not as a mere concept but as an intuition (apprehension of the object itself)—if I can make this credible, I have a great advantage over those who must first justify themselves before they are allowed to celebrate the truth of their assertions. I can henceforth speak in the tone of a lord who is so lofty as to be exempted from the burden of proving the title of his property (*beati possidentes*).—Long live philosophy drawn from feelings, a philosophy that leads us directly to the things themselves! Away with rational argumentation from concepts, which searches for things only through the detour of universal characteristics and which, before it even has the material that it can grasp immediately, demands determinate forms to which it can attribute that material! And, supposing also that reason can carry its explanations no further

---

equal to one another, because each is *everyone,* but also egalitarians who want everyone to equate one another, because they are all *nothing* outside of a One, and are monarchists out of envy; conscious of their own inability to think on their own, sometimes they exalt Plato on the throne and sometimes Aristotle in order not to suffer a despised comparison with those who are currently alive. And this is how the superior man (superior by his own admission) acts the philosopher: he brings all more distant philosophizing to an end through obfuscation.—This phenomenon could not be better presented in its proper light than in the fable of Voß (*Berlinische Monatsschrift,* November 1795, last page), a poem that is alone worth a hecatomb.

than determining the rightfulness of the acquisition of the insights that thus rise above reason, there still remains a fact: "philosophy has its secrets that *can be felt.*"[3]

[396] With the acceptance of a pregiven ability to feel an object that can still be encountered only in pure reason,

[3]A famous owner of such secrets expresses himself in this way: "To the extent that reason, as legislator of the will, must say to the phenomena (understood here, free actions of human beings), 'you please me—you displease me,' it must see these phenomena as effects of real things."[d] From this he concludes that the legislation of reason requires not only a *form* but also *matter* (content, purpose) as a determining ground of the will; that is, *a feeling of pleasure* (or displeasure) in an object *must precede* an action if reason is to be practical at all.—This error, which, if one lets it creep in the door, erases all morality and would leave nothing in its place but the maxim of happiness that cannot actually have any objective principle (because it varies according to the differences among subjects); this error, I say, can be securely brought to light only through the following *criterion of feeling.* The *pleasure* (or displeasure) that must necessarily precede the law in order for the act to take place is *pathological;* the pleasure or displeasure that the *law* has to precede in order for either one to be felt is, on the other hand, *moral.* The former one has empirical principles (the matter of the elective will), the latter a pure principle a priori at its foundation (wherein it simply concerns the form of the determination of the will).—Here the deceptive conclusion (*fallacia causae non causae*) can easily be discovered, since the eudemon alleges that the pleasure (contentment) that a virtuous man has as a prospect, in order some day to feel it in the consciousness [396] of his well-led life (and therefore to have the prospect of his future *happiness*) *is indeed the actual motivating force* behind the way he leads his life (according to the law). For, since I must at first assume that this man is virtuous and obeys the law in order to feel in the future a pleasure in the consciousness of his well-led life, any conclusion that makes the latter, which is a *consequence,* into the *cause* of his well-led life is the result of purely circular argumentation.

As for the *syncretism* of some moralists who make *eudemonism,* if not into the entire principle of morality, then at least into a part of this principle (if one yet admits that this eudemonism also has, without the subject having any awareness, influence on the deter-

things take a peculiar turn. Up until now, one has heard of *three* levels of assent [*Fürwahrhalten*], after which it disappears into complete uncertainty: knowledge, belief, and opinion.[4] Now a new level of assent is proposed [397]—a level that has nothing to do with logic, that is not supposed

---

mination of the human will that corresponds with duty): this syncretism is precisely the way to be without any principles. For the motivating forces that, deriving from happiness, intervene in the determination of the will, even if they are indeed efficacious in precisely those *actions* that flow from purely moral principles, nevertheless make the moral *disposition* impure and weak at the same time; the value and high rank of this disposition consists in demonstrating, without concern for these motivating forces and indeed by overcoming all their commendations, strict obedience to nothing but the law.

[4]Sometimes one uses the intermediate word in the theoretical sense as being equivalent in meaning with this latter: holding something for *probable;* and it must here be noted that it cannot be said of that which lies beyond the limits of all possible knowledge that it is *probable,* nor that it is *improbable,* and therefore even the word *faith* with respect to such an object in its *theoretical meaning* is not appropriate.—Under the expression "This or that is *probable,*" one understands something intermediate (in assent) between opinion and knowledge; and so it goes with all intermediate things, all things in the middle: one does with them *what one wants.*—If, however, someone says, for example, "It is at least *probable* that the soul lives after death," the speaker does not know what he wants.[e] For *probable* means "that which is held to be true and given assent," since it has more certainty (sufficient reason) on it side. The reasons must therefore contain partial knowledge, a part of the *cognition* of the object that has been judged. If, therefore, the object is absolutely not an object of knowledge possible for us (such is the case for the nature of the soul as living substance outside of its connection to the body, that is, as spirit), then the possibility [397] of such knowledge can be judged neither probable nor improbable; it cannot be judged at all. For the supposed grounds of knowledge reside in a series that does not approach a sufficient reason and therefore knowledge itself, since it refers to something super-

to register progress in understanding but is rather the presentiment (*praevisio sensitiva*) of that which is absolutely not an object of the senses: that is, the *intimation* [Ahnung] of the supersensible.[5]

[398] It is immediately apparent that intimation consists

---

sensible about which, as supersensible, no theoretical knowledge is possible.

Nothing changes with the belief in someone else's *testimony* concerning something supersensible.[f] The assent of a testimonial is always something empirical; and the person whom I am supposed to believe on the basis of his testimony must be an object of experience. But if this person were taken as a supersensible being, then experience can teach me nothing about his very existence, hence, not even that there is such a being who testifies to me (for it is contradictory to assert that experience can teach something about the supersensible); from the subjective impossibility of my inability to explain the appearance of a call interiorized in me, I cannot even draw the conclusion that this call comes from nowhere but a supersensible influence (as a consequence of what was said above concerning judgments of probability). Thus, there is no theoretical belief in the supersensible.

In a practical (moral-practical) sense, however, a belief in the supersensible is not only possible; it is even indissociably bound up with moral practice. For the sum of morality in me, although supersensible and therefore not empirical, is nevertheless given with unmistakable truth and authority (by a categorical imperative), but it commands an end (the highest good), which, from a theoretical perspective, cannot be accomplished through my capacities alone without a power of a world-master [*Weltherrscher*] exerting an effect on it. But to *believe* in him in a practical-moral manner does not mean to begin by assuming his reality as true from a theoretical perspective so that one could receive enlightenment about the end commanded as well as the motor-springs to bring this end into effect, for the law of reason is already objectively sufficient for this purpose; rather, to believe in a practical-moral manner is to act in accordance with the ideal of that end as if such a world-government is real, because that imperative (which commands not the belief but rather the action) contains on the part of man obein a certain mysterious rhythm [*mystischer Takt*], a vaulting leap (*salto mortale*) beyond concepts into the unthinkable, a capacity to grasp what evades every concept, an expectation of secrets or, rather, a suspense-ridden tendering of secrets that is actually the mistuning of heads into exaltation [*Verstimmung der Köpfe zur Schwärmerei*]. For intimation is obscure preexpectation and contains the hope of a disclosure that is only possible in tasks of reason solved with concepts; if, therefore, those intimations are transcendent and can lead to no proper *cognition* of the object, they must necessarily promise a surrogate of cognition,[6] supernatural communication (mystical illumination), which is then the death of all philosophy.

Plato the *academic* was, therefore, although it was not his fault (for he used his intellectual intuitions only backward, to *explain* the possibility of synthetic knowledge a priori, not forward, to *widen* this knowledge through such intuition into Ideas readable in the divine intellect), the father of all exaltation in *philosophy.* But I would not at all want to confuse Plato the *letter writer* (newly translated into German) with Plato the academic. The letter writer wants beyond "the four things belonging to knowledge—the *name* of the object, the *description,* the *presentation,* and the *science*—still a *fifth* [wheel on the wagon—insertion of I. Kant], namely, the

---

dience and subjection to his *power of choice* [Willkür] under the law, but it also contains in the part of the *will* [Willen] that commands to him this end a faculty (which is not human) adequate to this end, a faculty on whose behalf human reason can indeed command actions but not the success of actions (the achievement of the end), since success is not always or entirely in the power of man. It is therefore in the categorical imperative of practical reason according to its matter—an imperative that says, "I will that your action harmonize with the final purpose of all things"—that the presupposition of a legislating will [*gesetzgebenden Willen*] is already at the same time thought, a will that contains all power (of the divine) and that does not need to be urged in any special way.

object itself and *its true being*." "This immutable essence that can only be intuited in the soul and by the soul in which, for its part, as from a jetting spark of fire, a light ignites on its own—this essence is what he [the exalted philosopher—insertion of I. Kant] wishes to have grasped; one can nevertheless not speak of this essence, at least not to the people, since one would immediately be transported because of ignorance; since every attempt of this kind would already be dangerous, partly because of the crude contempt to which these higher truths are exposed, partly [which is here only reasonable—insertion of I. Kant] because the soul may be strained into empty hopes and into vain delusions of knowing great secrets."[7]

Who does not see here the mystogogue—the one who does not merely rave on his own but at the same time is a club member and, when he speaks to his disciples, in contrast to the people (among whom all uninitiated are to be counted), acts *superior* with his supposed philosophy! Let me bring out some new examples.

In the new mystical-Platonic language the following is said: "All philosophy [399] of man can only sketch the dawn; the sun must be intimated."[8] But indeed no one can intimate the sun if he has never seen one before. For it could very well happen that, on our globe, days regularly followed nights (as in the Mosaic story of creation) without one ever attaining a view of the sun because of constantly overcast skies, and all activities would nevertheless take their proper course according to this change (of the days and the seasons). In such circumstances a true philosopher would certainly not *intimate* a sun (for that is not his concern) but would nevertheless perhaps be able to make a *guess* in order to explain that phenomenon by assuming a hypothesis of such a heavenly body, and could, with luck, hit upon precisely this phenomenon. Indeed, to look into the sun (the supersensible) without becoming blind is impossible. But to see, as the elder Plato did, this sun in *reflection* (of reason morally illuminating the soul) and, indeed, to do so sufficiently from a practical point of view is entirely possible. In contrast, the Neo-Platonics "certainly give us a theatrical sun," because they want to confuse us by means of feelings (intimations), which are merely subjective and give absolutely no concept of the object, in order to hold us in suspense with the delusion of objective knowledge that takes off for extravagant places beyond.—The Platonizing philosophy of feelings never exhausts its supply of such figural expressions [*bildlichen Ausdrücken*], which are supposed to make that intimation comprehensible; for example, "to approach so near the goddess wisdom that one can perceive the *rustle* of her garment," but also in the praising of the art of *pseudo-Plato,* "since he cannot lift up the veil of Isis, he can nevertheless make it so thin that one can *intimate* the goddess under this veil."[9] Precisely how thin is not said; presumably, just thick enough so that one can make the specter into whatever one wants. For otherwise it would be a vision that should definitely be avoided.

For the purpose of argumentation, since there is a lack of rigorous proofs, the following are offered as arguments: "analogies, probabilities" (which were discussed above), thus "the danger of emasculating [*Entmannung*] a faculty of reason that has become so high-strung by metaphysical[5] subli-

[5]What the Neo-Platonic has spoken up until now is, to the extent that it concerns the treatment of his theme, pure *metaphysics* and can therefore only concern the formal principles of reason. But it also surreptitiously substitutes for this a *hyperphysics,* that is, not various principles of practical reason but a theory concerning the *nature* of the supersensible (of God, the human spirit), and [400] it claims to know that this web is "not so very finely" woven. Just how *absolutely empty* a philosophy that touches on the matter (the object) of pure rational concepts is, once it (as in transcendental theology) has been carefully detached from all empirical threads, can be seen in the following example.

The transcendental concept of God, as the *most real* being of all, cannot be avoided in philosophy, however abstract it may be. For it belongs to the binding and at the same time to the purification of all concrete concepts that are able afterward to enter into applied

mation [*metaphysische Sublimation*] that it [400] can hardly maintain itself in the struggle with vice,"[10] whereas it is in precisely these a priori principles that practical reason rightly feels its otherwise never intimated strength, and it is, on the other hand, in falsely attributed empirical properties

---

theology and the doctrine of religion. Now the question arises: should I think of God as the *totality* (complexus, aggregatum) of all realities or as their ultimate *ground*? If I choose the first, I must give examples of this material from which I put together the highest being so that its concept will not be altogether empty and without meaning. I will therefore attribute to this being something like an *understanding,* or also a *will* and the like, as realities. But every understanding with which I am familiar is a faculty of *thinking,* that is, a discursive capacity to have representations, or an understanding that operates by characteristics that several things have in common (from whose *differences* I therefore must abstract in thought) and, hence, is impossible without the subject being *limited.* Consequently, a divine understanding is not to be assumed from a faculty of thinking. But I have not the slightest concept of another kind of understanding, one that would be a faculty of intuition; consequently, the concept of an understanding that I posit in the highest being is completely without meaning. And yet, if I posit in this being another reality, a *will,* through which it is the cause of all things outside itself, I must assume a will in which its satisfaction (*acquiescentia*) does not thoroughly depend on the existence of things outside itself, for that would be a limitation (*negatio*). Now, I have, once again, not the slightest concept and cannot give a single example of a will in which the subject does not base its satisfaction on the *success* of its will and therefore of a will that does not *depend* on the existence of external objects. The concept of a will belonging to the highest being, as a reality inhering in it, is just as empty as the preceding concept, or it is (and this is even worse) an anthropomorphic concept that, once drawn into practical matters, which is inevitable, corrupts all religion and turns it into idolatry. If, on the other hand, I make from the *ens realissimum* the concept of the *ground* of all reality, I then say: God is the being that contains the ground of everything in the world, *in addition to which we human beings are forced to assume an intellect* (e.g., for everything purposive in [401] the world); it is the being from which the existence of every

(which are, for this exact reason, unfit for universal legislation) that reason is emasculated and crippled [*entmannet und gelähmt*].

---

[401] Finally, the most recent German wisdom exposes its exhortation *to philosophize by feeling* (not, as it was several

---

worldly being has its origin, not from the necessity of its *nature* (*per emanationem*) but in accordance with a relationship for which *we human beings* must assume *a free will* in order to make the possibility of this relationship comprehensible to us. Now, in this case, what the *nature* of the highest being (objectively) is can be entirely unfathomable to us and indeed can be posited entirely beyond the sphere of all theoretical knowledge we are able to attain, and yet this concept can nevertheless maintain (subjective) reality *in a practical respect* (to a way of life); only in relation to this reality can an *analogy* of the divine intellect and the divine will with that of man and his practical reason be assumed, whereas theoretical considerations of the relation between the divine and the human reserve no place for analogy. The concept of God, which pure practical reason compels us *to make ourselves,* proceeds from the moral law that our own reason prescribes to us with authority, not from the theory of the nature of things in themselves.

If, therefore, one of these strong men who have recently proclaimed with great enthusiasm a wisdom that costs them no effort because they pretend to have seized this goddess at the tip of her garment and to have brought her into their power says, "I have contempt for whoever thinks *to make for himself his God,*"[g] this speech then belongs to the peculiarities of his caste, whose tone (by virtue of a special favor) is *superior.* For it is altogether clear that we ourselves must make a concept that has to proceed from our reason. Had we wished to obtain it from some appearance (from an object of experience), our basis of knowledge would then be empirical and would therefore be unfit for universal validity, hence for apodictic practical certainty, which a universally obligatory law must have. We would have to confront a wisdom that personally appeared to us with a concept, as archetype, that we ourselves made in order to see whether this person also corresponded to the character of the archetype we made ourselves; and even if we did

years ago, to *strengthen* and motivate moral *feeling* by philosophy) to a test that it cannot help but lose. Its challenge is expressed in this way: "The surest mark by which the genuineness of human philosophy can be recognized is not that it makes us more certain [402] but that it makes us *better*."[11] One cannot demand of this test that the betterment of man (effected by a secret feeling) be attested by an assay-master who cupels its morality. For indeed everyone can easily attest to the standard of good actions, but when it is a matter of determining how on the mark these actions are in intention and attitude, who can give an account of them that has *public validity*? And it would have to be such an account if it is going to be used to prove that feeling in general makes better human beings, whereas scientific theory is fruitless and ineffective.[12] No experience, moreover, can deliver a touchstone; it must be sought, rather, only in practical reason, as given a priori. Inner experience as well as feeling (which is in itself empirical and thus contingent) is stirred only by the voice of reason (*dictamen rationis*), which clearly speaks to everyone and is capable of being known scientifically; a particular practical rule is not, however, introduced for reason by some kind of feeling, which is impossible, because that rule could never be universally valid. One must therefore be able to perceive a priori exactly which principle can make human beings better, provided that one bring this principle clearly and incessantly before their souls and pay attention to the powerful impression it makes on them.

---

not encounter anything in this person that contradicted this archetype, it is nevertheless absolutely impossible to know its adequacy with regard to the archetype without a supersensible experience (because the object is supersensible), and this is self-contradictory. *Theophany* therefore makes an *idol* from Plato's Idea, and this idol can be honored only superstitiously; in contrast, *theology*, which proceeds from the concepts of our own reason, sets up an *Ideal*,[h] which compels us into worship, since it itself arises from the most sacred duties that are themselves independent of theology.

Now, every human being finds in reason the Idea of duty, and trembles as he listens to its adamant voice when inclinations, which try to make him deaf and disobedient to this voice, arise within him. He is convinced that if all these inclinations conspire to unite against the voice of reason and yet the majesty of the law, which his own reason prescribes to him, must nevertheless and without hesitation outweigh them all, then his will is also capable of doing so.[13] Even if it is not done in a scientific manner, all this can and must be clearly presented to a human being, so that they may be certain of the authority of his reason, as it bids him to act, and be sure of the authority of the commands that reason issues; and so much for theory. Now, I consider a man as he asks himself: What is in me that makes it so that I can sacrifice the most inner allurements of my drives and all the desires that proceed from my nature to a law that promises me no advantage as a replacement and threatens no loss if it is transgressed; indeed, a law that I honor all the more inwardly the more strictly it bids and the less it offers in return? This question stirs up the entire soul through the astonishment over the greatness and sublimity of the inner disposition [403] of humanity and at the same time the impenetrability of the secret that it conceals (for the answer—it is *freedom*—would be tautological, precisely because freedom constitutes the secret itself). One cannot become tired of directing one's attention toward it and admiring in oneself a power that yields to no power of nature; and this admiration is precisely the feeling generated from Ideas that make human beings morally *better* if, beyond the doctrines of morals taught by schools and pulpits, the presentation of this secret still constituted a frequently repeated occupation of the teacher, if it penetrated deeply into the soul and was not neglected.

Here is what Archimedes needed but did not find: a firm point on which reason can set down its lever, and indeed it is neither in the present nor in a future world that he needed to set it down but, rather, in reason's inner Idea of freedom, which, on account of the unshakable moral law, stands there as a secure foundation for setting the human will into motion by its principles, even against the opposition of nature in its entirety. Such is the secret that *can be felt* only after a long development of concepts of the understanding and carefully tested principles, thus only through work.—It is not empirically given (set up for rational analysis) but is given a priori (as an actual insight within the limits of our reason), and it even widens rational knowledge to the supersensible, but only from a practical point of view: not by some sort of *feeling* that grounds knowledge (the mystical) but by clear *knowledge* that acts on feeling (moral feeling).—The tone of those who believe themselves in possession of this true secret cannot be superior. For only dogmatic or historical knowledge puffs up. Dogmatic knowledge lowers its voice through the critique of its own rationality, and its claims are inevitably forced into moderation (modesty); as for the presumptuousness of historical knowledge, being well-read in Plato and the classics belongs only to the culture of taste [*Kultur des Geschmacks*] and thus does not justify wanting to use such reading to act the philosopher.

To reproach this claim did not seem to me to be superfluous in our times, when ornamentation with the title of philosophy has become a fashionable item, and the philosopher of *vision* (if one admits such a thing), because it is so easy to attain the peak of insight by a bold leap without effort, can surreptitiously gather a great following [404] around himself (for boldness is contagious)—a phenomenon that the police in the realm of the sciences cannot tolerate.

The disparaging way of denouncing *formulations* in our knowledge (which is indeed the principal activity of philosophy) as pedantry under the name of "form-giving manufacture"[14] confirms the suspicion of a secret intention: in fact to ban all philosophy under the shop-sign of philosophy, and to act superior as the victor over philosophy (*pedibus subiecta vicissim obteritur, nos exaequat victoria coelo,* Lucretius[15]).—But how little this attempt can succeed under the illumination of an ever increasing critique is visible from the following example.

The essence of a thing consists in its form (*forma dat esse rei,* as the Scholastics said) insofar as this essence is supposed to be known by reason. If this thing is an object of the senses, its form is in intuition (as appearances), and indeed pure mathematics is nothing other than a theory of form for pure *intuition;* metaphysics as well as pure philosophy grounds its knowledge, above all, in *forms of thought* under which every object (matter of knowledge) may be afterward subsumed. The possibility of all synthetic knowledge a priori rests on these forms, and the fact that we have this knowledge cannot be disputed. But the passage to the supersensible toward which reason irresistibly drives us and which it can accomplish only from a moral-practical point of view—this passage reason itself produces only by those (practical) laws that make the matter of free actions (their purpose) not into their principle but, rather, into only their form, the fitness of their maxims for universal legislation in general. In both fields (the theoretical, the practical) there is no arbitrary *form-giving* set up (on the behalf of the State) in accordance with a *plan* or an *industry,* but there is a *manufacture* that handles, above all, the object given; and indeed, without a preconceived thought, there is an ever proceeding labor and careful work of the subject to take up and appraise its own faculty (of reason); in contrast, the gentleman, as a man of honor, who opens up an oracle for the vision of the supersensible cannot deny having installed it for a mechanical treatment of heads [*mechanische Behandlung der Köpfe*] and having given such treatment the name of philosophy only as an honorific title.

---

[405] But what is the good of all this conflict between two parties that at bottom share one and the same intention: to make people wise and virtuous? It is much noise about noth-

ing, disunity out of a misunderstanding in which no reconciliation but only a reciprocal clarification is needed in order to conclude a treaty that makes future concord even more heartfelt.

The veiled goddess before whom we of both parties bend our knees is the moral law in us, in its inviolable majesty. We do indeed perceive her voice and also understand very well her command. But when we are listening, we are in doubt whether it comes from man, from the perfected power of his own reason, or whether it comes from an other, whose essence is unknown to us and speaks to man through this, his own reason. At bottom we would perhaps do better to rise above and thus spare ourselves research into this matter; since such research is only speculative and since what obliges us (objectively) to act remains always the same, one may place one or the other principle down as a foundation. But the didactic procedure of bringing the moral law within us into clear concepts according to a logical methodology is the only authentically *philosophical* one, whereas the procedure whereby the law is personified and reason's moral bidding is made into a veiled Isis (even if we attribute to her no other properties than those discovered according to the method above), is an *aesthetic* mode of representing precisely the same object; one can doubtless use this mode of representation backward, after the first procedure has already purified the principles, in order to enliven those ideas by a sensible, albeit only analogical, presentation, and yet one always runs the danger of falling into an exalting vision [*schwärmerische Vision*], which is the death of all philosophy.

To be able to *intimate* that goddess would therefore be an expression that means nothing more than to be led to concepts of duty by moral *feeling* before one could have *clarified* the principles on which this feeling depends; such an intimation of a law, as soon as methodical treatment lets it pass into clear insight, is the authentic occupation of philosophy without which the expression of reason would be the voice of an *oracle*[6] that is exposed to all sorts of interpretations.

[406] As for the rest, "if," as Fontenelle says on another occasion, without taking this suggestion for an agreement, "Mr. N. still wants to believe in oracles, no one can prevent him from doing so."[16]

Königsberg I. Kant

Notes on the Text

This essay first appeared in the journal *Berlinische Monatsschrift* 27 (May 1796): 387–426. The principal object of Kant's polemic is the annotated translation of Plato by Johann Georg Schlosser, *Platos Briefe über die syrakusanische Staatsrevolution, nebst einer historischen Einleitung und Anmerkung* (Plato's letters on the revolution in Syracuse with a historical introduction and notes) (Königsberg: F. Ni-

---

[6]This business of secrecy has a way all its own. Its adepts make no secret of having had their light ignited by Plato, [406] and this purported Plato freely admits that if one asks him what this light consists of (what is clarified by it), he does not know what to say. So much the better! For it is self-evident that he—another Prometheus—has snatched the sparks for this fire directly from heaven. So one does well to speak in a superior tone if one is from old, hereditary nobility and can say, "In our prematurely aged times, whatever is spoken or done out of feeling is considered to be enthusiastic exaltation. Poor Plato, if you did not have the seal of antiquity about you and if one could claim to be a scholar without having read you, who would still want to read you in this *prosaic* age in which the highest wisdom is to see nothing but what lies at our feet and to assume nothing but what we can grasp with our hands?"[i] But this conclusion unfortunately does not follow; it proves too much. For *Aristotle,* an extremely prosaic philosopher, certainly has the seal of antiquity about him, and according to the principle stated above, he has a claim to being read!—At bottom, all philosophy is indeed prosaic; and the suggestion that we should now start to philosophize poetically would be just as welcome as the suggestion that a businessman should in the future no longer write his account books in prose but rather in verse.

colovius, 1795); the lengthy endnote to this rare volume has been reprinted in an essay of Ingegrete Kreienbrink, "Johann Georg Schlossers Streit mit Kant" in *Festschrift für Detlev W. Schumann zum 70. Geburtstag,* ed. Albert R. Schmitt (Munich: Delp, 1970) 247–48. J. G. Schlosser (1739–99), is best known as Goethe's brother-in-law, having married Cornelia von Goethe and, after her death, Goethe's friend Johanna Fahlmer. Schlosser was an eclectic writer who cultivated a florid style in which Christian sentimentalism joined with quotations from classical authors in order to support a "dogmaticism" (his own term) on whose basis a harmonious society was to be maintained. The major activities of "the good Schlosser" (Goethe) were devoted to administrative duties. In 1773 he became a governmental secretary in Treptow; afterward, he was a privy councilor in Karlsruhe, and a high official in Emmindingen, Ansbruch, and Eutin (Baden). Upon retirement from governmental service (1794), he devoted himself to writing. His principal literary achievements were translations of Plato, all of which were soon eclipsed by the incomparable translations of his one-time student, Friedrich Schleiermacher.

Schlosser's relation to Goethe lent him a certain fame, and he himself induced divergent reactions in a wide range of acquaintances, many of which were highly unfavorable. His political views were in general hierarchical, feudal, and reactionary. It is no accident that in 1795 Schlosser decided to translate the disputed letters of Plato concerning the failed revolution in Syracuse, for his aim was clearly to demonstrate the futility and bankruptcy of revolutionary politics; that these letters also discussed the possibility of attaining insight into things themselves and, in turn, pleaded for a restriction on the discussion of this insight contributed to Schlosser's aristocratic and starkly antirevolutionary opinions. To this extent, he does not belong to the ones who were "enthusiastic" (Kant's word) about the revolution and indeed communicated this enthusiasm even when they understood the dangers they faced. So long as this enthusiasm could be shown to be *universal,* it constituted, according to Kant, the "historical sign" (*Geschichtszeichen*) that allowed him to read the future of the human race and declare with confidence that it was constantly progressing toward the better.

It is quite possible that Kant was drawn to combat Schlosser, an unworthy opponent of the philosopher who had written the *Critique of Pure Reason,* because he was a glaring exception to this universal enthusiasm and, to this extent, stood in the way of Kant's reading of the "historical sign." Schlosser's desire to insinuate himself into the aristocracy and his tactic of assuming the airs of the nobility would at least make it comprehensible why he was so unenthusiastic about the establishment of a constitutional government in France (see Kant's essay "Renewed Question: Is the Human Race Constantly Progressing Toward the Better?" first published in 1798 as the second section of *The Conflict of the Faculties,* intro. Mary J. Gregor, trans. Mary J. Gregor and Robert E. Anchor [New York: Abaris, 1979]; cf. the analysis of the terms of Kant's "conflict" in Jacques Derrida, "Mochlos ou le conflit des facultés," *Du droit à la philosophie* [Paris: Galilée, 1990], 397–438). As the "Renewed Question" makes clear, nothing could be more an anathema to Kant than a statement Schlosser wrote on the eve of the Revolution: "But it should be said to the people: however unjust their kings were when they did with them what they wanted and however much these kings would be punished for it, the people nevertheless cannot have the right to complain until things on their side are also set again in the relations of nature" (*Seuthes oder der Monarch* [Straßburg: Akademische Buchhandlung, 1788], 149).

A sympathetic and fully developed sketch of Schlosser's life and thought can be found in Detlev W. Schumann's lengthy introduction to his minor writings, Johann Georg Schlosser, *Kleine Schriften* (1779–93; reprint, New York: Johnson Reprint Corp., 1972), vol. 1.

Schlosser was not the only target—nor was he the only translator of Plato—against whom Kant aimed his polemic. According to Heinz Heimsoeth, there was a widespread "Plato-enthusiasm" during the 1790s, and Kant set out to combat its deleterious effects (see Heimsoeth, "Plato in Kants Werdegang" in *Studien zur Kants philosophischen Entwicklung,* eds. H. Heimsoeth, D. Henrich, and G. Tonelli [Hildesheim: Olms, 1967], 124–43). Although it never mentions him by name, Kant's attack is just as sharply aimed at the notes written by another translator of Plato, Count Friedrich Leopold zu Stolberg, *Auserlesene Gespräche des Platon* (Königsberg: F. Nicolivius, 1796). Count Stolberg (1750–1819), who is perhaps best known for his enthusiasm for Shakespeare and for the controversy surrounding his conversion to Catholicism in 1800, drew Schlosser into his circle of friends, all of whom were committed to a kind of Christian sentimentalism. Like Schlosser, Stolberg presented Socrates as a victim of democracy and, above all, as a forerunner of Jesus.

It is no mere coincidence—and indeed, indicates the extent of the constellation in which Kant and Goethe formed the extreme points—that Goethe, entirely independently of Kant, vehemently rejected Stolberg's preface to his edition of Plato. Goethe employs the same polemical strategy, the same "irony," and even the very same words as Kant when he attacks Stolberg. In a letter to Schiller, Goethe called the preface "a slovenly work," and in a letter to Wilhelm von Humbolt, he simply described it as "monstrous" (letter of 3 December, 1795, *Goethes Briefe,* ed. K. R. Mandelkow [Hamburg: Wegner, 1964], 2:208); indeed, he was so incensed that he wrote (although he did not immediately publish) an extraordinary rejoinder, "Plato als Mitgenosse einer christlichen Offenbarung: Im Jahre 1796 durch eine Uebersetzung veranlaßt" (Plato as comrade of a Christian revelation: Occasioned in 1796 by a translation), a brief essay that was not published until 1826, several years after Stolberg's death; see *Goethes Werke* (Hamburg: Wegner, 1953), 11:244–49. Goethe's essay, like Kant's, is chiefly concerned with the "enthusiasm" that consumed Christian sentimentalists, and it not only argues for an ironic Plato—a Plato who distances himself from the very enthusiasm he generates—but also enacts this irony in its treatment of Stolberg's exaltation. Goethe even uses the word *vornehm* ("superior") when he points out how deeply Stolberg wants to exempt himself from labor in order to puff himself up. At issue is the question raised in the *Ion,* namely, how to explain the sudden emergence of poetic talent: "Even the recognized poet is capable only at certain moments of showing his talent in the highest degree, and one can investigate this effect of human spirit psychologically, without having recourse to miracles and strange happenings, if one possesses enough patience to follow the natural phenomena whose knowledge is offered to us in science; it is, of course, easier to look away in a superior manner [*vornehm*] than to esteem what science accomplishes with insight and reasonableness" (*Goethes Werke,* 11:248).

Kant's essay was reprinted, apparently without his permission, in Johann Georg Schlosser, *Schreiben an einen jungen Mann, der die kritische Philosophie studieren wollte* (Lübeck and Leipzig: F. Bohn, 1797), 124–68. It set off a widespread discussion, which Kant himself tried to bring to a close with his "Announcement of the Near Conclusion of a Treaty for Perpetual Peace in Philosophy" (see my notes to this essay).

1. Kant himself was early on attracted to the problem of fire. If he was not precisely a *philosophus per ignem,* he was nevertheless a *philosophus de igne,* since his doctoral dissertation, written in 1755, was a meditation on fire; see Immanuel Kant, *Meditationum quarun-*

dam de igne succincta delineato, 1:399–84; trans. as "Succinct Exposition of Some Meditations on Fire," *Kant's Latin Writings,* trans. and ed. Lewis White Beck (New York: Peter Lang, 1986), 23–46. In another early work, Kant ponders the *spiritus rector,* as a "fifth essence," which lets one suppose a *Weltgeist* (world-spirit); see Kant, "Physical Consideration of the Question: Is the Earth Growing Old?" (1:211–12).

2. Kant's use of the word *dogmatic* should not be equated with the metaphysical dogmaticism against which the three *Critiques* were written. The preface to the second edition of the *Critique of Pure Reason* makes the following distinction: "This critique is not opposed to the *dogmatic procedure* of reason in its pure knowledge, as science, for that must always be dogmatic, that is, yield strict proof from sure principles a priori. It is opposed to *dogmaticism,* that is, to the presumption that it is possible to make progress with pure knowledge, according to principles, from concepts alone (those that are philosophical), as reason has long been in the habit of doing; and that it is possible to do this without having first investigated in what way and by what right reason has come into possession of these concepts. Dogmaticism is thus the dogmatic procedure of pure reason, *without previous criticism of its own powers*" (B xxxv). A system of "dogmata" ("synthetic propositions directly derived from concepts" [A 736; B 764]) can thus be developed after a thoroughgoing critique of the possibility of such propositions has been carried out. In a letter to L. H. Jakob on 11 September 1787, Kant writes: "My *Critique of Practical Reason* is at Grunet's now. It contains many things that will serve to correct the misunderstandings of the theoretical. I shall now turn at once to the 'Critique of Taste,' with which I shall have finished my critical work, so that I can proceed to the dogmatic part" (Kant, *Philosophical Correspondence,* ed. and trans. Arnulf Zweig [Chicago: University of Chicago Press, 1967], 125; 10:494). In Schlosser's second reply, he insists that he is a "dogmatist," not a "mystic" (see *Zweites Schreiben an einen jungen Mann, der die kritische Philosophie studieren wollte, veranlasst durch den angehängten Aufsatz des Herrn Professor Kant über den Philosophienfrieden* [Lübeck and Leipzig: F. Bohn, 1798], 20).

3. Kant is referring to the voluminous work of Jean-Etienne Montucla, *Histoire des mathématiques* (Paris: H. A. Agasse, 1758–1802).

4. This assertion concerning the rational relation of a right-angled triangle landed Kant in an unexpected conflict with the faculty of mathematics. Three months after this essay appeared, Jo-

hann Albrecht Heinrich Reimarus, professor of natural history in Hamburg, attacked Kant in a brief essay about such triangles (see "Ueber die rationalen Verhältnisse der drei Seiten eines rechtwinkligen Dreiecks," *Berlinische Monatsschrift* 28 [August 1796]: 145–49). Reimarus rightly maintained that there is an indefinite number of rational relations. Kant responded with a short letter to the journal entitled "Ausgleichung eines auf Mißverstand beruhenden mathematischen Streits" (Settlement of a mathematical conflict resting on a misunderstanding). In the essay, he maintains there can be no conflict at all: "Nothing appears to be clearer than the fact that we cannot conceive of a real mathematical conflict (which is almost unheard of). . . . The expression of each of the two [in the conflict] is taken in a different sense; as soon as one comes to an understanding, therefore, the conflict vanishes, and both sides are right" (8:409). Kant excuses himself by explaining that he meant the series of numbers that follow one upon the other, and in any case Reimarus's statement gave no encouragement to "a mysticist" (8:410). The difficulties Kant encountered in answering the younger Reimarus can be judged by the many drafts he wrote of his response (23:199–205). On this matter, see the discussion of Hans Saner, *Kant's Political Thought,* trans. E. B. Ashton (Chicago: University of Chicago Press, 1973), 188–90.

5. In § 33 of the *Anthropology* on "the capacity to see beforehand (*praevisio*)," Kant comments on the ambiguity of the word *ahnen:* "Recently an attempt has been made to distinguish between *ahnen* and *ahnden;* but *ahnen* is not a German word, and there remains only *ahnden.—Ahnden* means 'to bear in mind' [*gedenken*]. *Es ahndet mir* means 'I have a vague recollection of it'; *etwas ahnden* means to remember someone's action to his detriment (that is, to punish it). It is always the same concept, but applied differently" (7:187; *Anthropology from a Pragmatic Point of View,* trans. Mary Gregor [The Hague: Nijhoff, 1974], 60; on the history of the word, see W. Nieke "Ahnung," *Historisches Wörterbuch der Philosophie,* ed. J. Ritter [Basel and Stuttgart: Schwabe, 1971], 1:115–17). Kant does not concern himself with why a word whose meaning is so closely linked with remembrance should then designate a mode of *praevisio.*

6. The grammar of the text is garbled at this point. The translation, following the Akademie edition, is thus only a conjecture. Given Cassirer's reading, the translation would run: "if, therefore, those intimations are transcendent and can lead to no proper *cognition* of the object, a surrogate of cognition is necessarily promised."

7. All these quotations are from the notes to Schlosser's translation of Plato's letters. In his "Letter to a young man who wants to study critical philosophy" (see the discussion below), Schlosser accuses Kant of using "the trivial language of the people" when he speaks of a "fourth wheel" (*Schreiben an einen jungen Mann,* 80). Schlosser, obviously drawing on the allegorical language of the *Phaedrus,* insists that it is not a wheel "but a wing on the white horse that pulls the wagon, a wing on the wagon-leader himself."

8. See Schlosser, *Platos Briefe,* 191n.

9. See ibid. Kant himself had drawn on the figure of Isis in a key footnote to the section of the *Critique of Judgment* devoted to the powers constitutive of genius: "Perhaps nothing more sublime has ever been said, or a thought ever been expressed more sublimely, than in that inscription above the temple of *Isis* (Mother of Nature): 'I am all that is, that was, and that will be, and no mortal has lifted my veil.' *Segner* made use of this idea in an ingenious vignette prefixed to his *Naturlehre,* so as first to imbue the pupil, whom he was about to lead into this temple, with the sacred thrill that is meant to attune the mind to solemn attentiveness [*das Gemüt zu feierlicher Aufmerksamkeit stimmen soll*]" (*Critique of Judgment,* trans. Werner S. Pluhar [Indianapolis, Ind.: Hackett Publishing Co., 1987], 185; 5:317). Not only does the veil of Isis correspond to a certain *Stimmung* (mood, disposition) in which receptivity for knowledge overcomes all sensual modes of reception; it also makes such cognitive *Empfängnis* (reception, conception) into the precondition on *conception* in general: a unique situation of double "conceptivity" without insemination. No wonder Kant—and Schlosser as well—worries about emasculation at this point. The inscription below the veil of Isis, as the most sublime expression ever written, has a long history in Kant's own writing, beginning with *The One Possible Basis for a Demonstration of the Existence of God,* trans. Gordon Treash (New York: Abaris, 1979), 215; 2:151. On this motif, see Sarah Kofman, *Le Respect des femmes* (Paris: Galilée, 1982).

10. See Schlosser, *Platos Briefe,* 182–83n.

11. See ibid. 184n. Schlosser repeats this remark throughout his conflict with Kant, and it is on this point that he concludes his "Second letter to a student who wants to study critical philosophy" (see the discussion below).

12. Kant was always sceptical with regard to the power of introspection to discover the actual intentions of an action (or the "determination of the will" in acting); see Kant, *Foundations of the Metaphysics of Morals,* trans. Lewis White Beck (Indianapolis, Ind.:

Bobbs-Merrill, 1959), 23–24. But, according to a path that Kant himself sketched, this skepticism grew into despair. In the 1793 work on religion, the tendency of human beings to attribute good intentions to actions whose "determination of the will" is evil almost prompted him to characterize the species not simply as radically evil but as *absolutely* evil. For such a tendency indicates a certain *Bosheit* (devilishness). See Kant, *Religion within the Limits of Reason Alone,* trans. Theodore M. Greene and Hoyt H. Hudson (New York: Harper and Row, 1960), 33–34.

13. In the *Critique of Practical Reason,* Kant adduces an example of such trembling (*Zittern*): a man is ordered by his sovereign to make a false deposition against an honorable man on pain of death; see Kant, *The Critique of Practical Reason,* trans. Lewis White Beck (Indianapolis, Ind.: Bobbs-Merrill, 1956), 30.

14. See Schlosser, *Platos Briefe,* 183n.

15. See Lucretius, *De rerum natura:* "Quare religio pedibus subjecta vicissim / obteritur, nos exaequat victoria caelo" (1:78–79); "Therefore Religion in her turn has been hurled down, and is trodden beneath our feet; and victory has raised us to the sky" (Lucretius, *On Nature,* trans. Russel M. Geer [Indianapolis, Ind.: Bobbs-Merrill, 1965], 6, modified).

16. According to Heinrich Maier, editor of the Akademie edition, this citation is most likely from Gottsched's translation of Fontenelle's *History of Heathen Oracles:* "If P. Baltus wants to think the oracle thoroughly devilish, he can always do so" (see 8:513).

Notes on the Footnotes

a. Kant was often brought back to the question of "superior" or "noble" persons during the years of the French Revolution. It is hardly an accident that Schlosser, who was not a nobleman, is the principal object of Kant's polemic, whereas Count Stolberg is never once mentioned by name, even though he is quoted numerous times. In the "Doctrine of Right" (1797), Kant defines the nobility as "a class of persons who acquire their rank before they have merited it" (*The Metaphysical Elements of Justice,* trans. John Ladd [Indianapolis, Ind.: Bobbs-Merrill, 1965], 97; 6:329). He goes on to remark: "Furthermore, there is no reason to hope that they will merit it. To think so is pure fancy and quite unrealistic. . . . Inasmuch as it can be assumed that no man would throw away freedom, it is impossible that the general will of the people would consent to such a groundless prerogative, and therefore neither can the sovereign make it valid." In the Supplementary Explanations, Kant insists upon the *transient* character of hereditary nobility: "The nobility is a temporary confraternity authorized by the state; but it must adapt itself to the circumstances of the times" (137; 6:370). In one of his last writings, "On Book-Making" (1798), Kant takes issue with an essay of Justus Möser for suggesting in a review of his "On a Proverb" that hereditary privileges could indeed be justified (see 8:433). Finally, the section of the *Anthropology* devoted to "national character" diagnoses a particular German "mania" for laying out "a ladder between ruler and subject, each rung of which is labeled with the degree of esteem due it; and a man who has no trade, and so no *title* is, as we say, nothing. . . . In fact, this mania, as a painstaking care and need for methodical division, so that a whole can be grasped under one concept, reveals the limitation of the German's innate talent" (Kant, *Anthropology*, 181; 7:319).

b. See Friedrich Leopold Graf zu Stolberg, *Reise in Deutschland, der Schweiz, Italien und Sizilien* (Königsberg and Leipzig: F. Nicolovius, 1794), 2:238–40.

c. See Stolberg's preface to his translation of selected works of Plato, which has been collected in *Gesammalte Werke der Brüder Christian und Friedrich Leopold Grafen zu Stolberg* (Hamburg: Perthes and Besser, 1820–24), 17:v–vi. The preface begins with a letter from Schlosser and proceeds to discuss the meaning of Socrates' "inner voice," and concludes with an exclusion of every interpretation of Plato that is not essentially Christian: the martyrdom of Socrates is, namely, a forerunner of the Crucifixion.

d. See Schlosser's notes to *Platos Briefe*, 194, 182.

e. Although Schlosser's confused notions of probability are doubtless Kant's principal target in this passage, it is possible that Pascal's famous wager—and the conception of faith grounded on it—is also under attack. In the section on lying in the part of *The Metaphysics of Morals* concerned with the "doctrine of virtue," Kant astutely shows how an "inner lie" (i.e. self-deception) is an integral component of the "success" of Pascal's wager, that is, its ability to make someone believe in God and the afterlife (see Kant, *The Doctrine of Virtue*, trans. and intro. Mary J. Gregor [Philadelphia: University of Pennsylvania Press, 1964], 94).

f. For Kant's earlier and more detailed dispute over the meaning and content of rational faith, see his reckoning with Friedrich Heinrich Jacobi, "Was heißt: sich im Denken orientieren?" (8:131–47; trans. as "What Is Orientation in Thinking," Kant, *Political Writ-*

ings, ed. Hans Reiss, trans. H. B. Nisbet [Cambridge: Cambridge University Press, 1990], 237–49).

g. See Schlosser, *Platos Briefe,* 183. In Schlosser's "Letter to a young man who wants to study critical philosophy," he insists that Kant creates a concept of God in order to worship the concept, not God; see *Schreiben,* 68–72.

h. On the transformation of the "idea" into an "idol," see § 38 of the *Anthropology,* where the *facultas signatrix* is discussed: "To say, with Swedenborg, that the real phenomena of the world present to the senses are merely a *symbol* of an intelligible world hidden in reserve is *exaltation* [Schwärmerei]. But in exhibiting the concepts that are the essence of all religion—concepts (called Ideas) that belong to morality and so to pure reason—it is *enlightenment* to distinguish the symbolic from the intellectual (public worship from religion), the temporarily useful and necessary husk from the thing itself. Otherwise we exchange an *Ideal* (of pure practical reason) for an *Idol,* and miss the final end.—It is an indisputable fact that all peoples on earth have begun by making this mistake [*Vertauschung*]" (7:191–92; *Anthropology,* 65). This catastrophic exchange at the origin not only generates history; it governs the rules of interpretation and therefore of substitution in general. On the basis of these rules the difference between *ideal* and *idol* is supposed to be readable.

i. See Schlosser, *Platos Briefe,* 90n.

Announcement of the Near Conclusion of a Treaty for Eternal Peace in Philosophy

* * *

First Part
Joyful Prospect of a Near Eternal Peace

From the Lowest Level of the Living Nature of Man to His Highest, Philosophy

Chryssipus says with characteristically Stoic force of language[1]: "Nature has endowed the pig with a *soul* instead of *salt* so that the pig would not *putrefy*." Such is the lowest level of human nature prior to all culture, namely, mere animal instinct.—But it is as if the philosopher has here cast a soothsayer's glance into the physiological systems of our time; only now one prefers to use the word *life-force* [*Lebenskraft*] rather than the word *soul* (and one is right to do so, since a *force* can indeed be inferred from an effect, but an immediate inference to a particular *substance* appropriate for this kind of effect cannot be made); one posits *life*, however, in the *action* of stimulating forces (vital stimulation) and in the capacity *to react* to stimulating forces (vital capacity), and one calls that person *healthy* in whom a proportional stimulation produces neither an excessive nor a deficient effect. In default of such health, the *animal* operation of nature passes over into a *chemical* one whose consequence is putrefaction, so that the putrefaction does not (as one otherwise thought) have to arise from and after death but, rather, death arises from the preceding putrefaction. Here

[1] Cicero, *De natura deorum*, bk. 2, § 160.[a]

the *nature* in man is represented prior to his humanity, therefore in its universality, as it is active in the animal only in order to develop forces that afterward can be applied according to laws of freedom. This activity and its activation is, however, not practical but still only mechanical.

A. On the Physical Causes of Human Philosophy

[414] If one *disregards* the one property that distinguishes man from all other animals—*self-consciousness* by virtue of which he is a *rational* animal (to whom, because of the unity of consciousness, only *one* soul can be attributed as well)—there is then the *propensity* to use this faculty of reason for *sophistical ratiocination* [*Vernünfteln*] in a methodical way and indeed to reason merely with concepts, that is, to *philosophize;* thus to grate others polemically with one's philosophy, that is, to *dispute,* and because this cannot easily take place without emotion, to *bicker* in favor of this philosophy and, finally, once united into a huge mass, to *lead an open war* against one another (school against school as army against army): this propensity, I say, or rather *impulse,* must be seen as one of the benevolent and wise arrangements of nature through which it seeks to avert men from a great misfortune, the putrefaction of the living body.[1]

On the Physical Effect of Philosophy

It is the *health* (*status salubritatis*) of reason, as an effect of philosophy. Since, however, human health (according to the statements above) is an incessant cycle of illness and convalescence, it has not yet come to terms with the mere *diet* of practical reason (a gymnastics of reason, so to speak) in order to maintain the balance that is called health and that hovers on the tip of a hair; rather, philosophy must act (therapeutically) as a *remedy* (*materia medica*) for whose use, then, dispensaries and doctors (the latter, however, are entitled to *order* the use) are required; here, the police must also be on watch so that those who arrogate to themselves the task of *recommending which philosophy one should study* are doctors trained in their discipline and not mere amateurs or quacks who bungle around in an art of which they do not even know the first elements.[2]

The Stoic philosopher *Posidonius* gave an example of the medicinal power of philosophy when he experimented on his very own person in the presence of the great Pompei (Cicero, *Tusculanes,* lib. 2, sect. 61[3]): he was able to overpower a violent attack of gout by means of a lively attack on the Epicurean school; the attack of gout went down to his feet [415], never having been able to reach his heart and his head. And so he proved the immediate *physical effect* of philosophy, which nature intended to achieve by its means (bodily health) when he declaimed the sentence: *pain is nothing evil.*[2]

[2]The ambiguity in the expression "bad" (*malum* [*Uebel*]) and "evil" (*pravum* [*Böse*]) is easier to avoid in Latin than in Greek. With respect to well-being and bad things (pains), human beings (like all sensible beings) stand under the law of *nature,* and are merely passive; with respect to *evil* (and good), man stands under the law of *freedom.* The former contains that which he *suffers;* the latter, that which he willingly *does.* With respect to *fate,* the difference between *right* and *left* (*fato vel dextro vel sinistro*) is a mere difference in the external relation of man. With respect to his freedom, however, and to the relation of the law to his inclinations, it is a difference in the interior of man. In the first case, the *straight* is opposed to the *slanting* (*rectum obliquo*); in the second case, the straight is opposed to the *crooked,* the crippled (*rectum pravo s. varo, obtorto*).[b]

The fact that the Latins assign an unfortunate event to the left side may very well arise because one is not as agile at warding off attacks with the left hand as with the right. But the reason that, in the auguries, when the *auspex* turned his face to the so-called *tempel* (in the south), he interpreted the lightning bolt that occurred on the left as good fortune seems to be that the thunder god who would be thought to be across from the *auspex* held his lightning in the right hand.

On the Illusion of the Incompatibility of Philosophy with a Lasting State of Peace for Philosophy

Dogmaticism (e.g., of the Wolffian school) is a cushion for going to sleep, and it is the end of all liveliness, which is precisely the benevolent aspect of philosophy. *Scepticism,* which constitutes the exact counterpart to dogmaticism when it is fully laid out, has nothing with which it can exercise an influence that would make reason stir. *Moderatism,* which takes its cue from the division between the two, is of the opinion that the philosopher's stone can be found in subjective *probability* and is under the delusion that piling up many isolated reasons (none of which is held to be demonstrative in its own right) can replace the lack of a sufficient reason and is therefore absolutely not a philosophy. This remedy (doxology) ends up like drops for the plague or like Venetian treacle: because *too much* is poured into them left and right, they *are good for nothing.*

On the Actual Compatibility of Critical Philosophy with a Lasting State of Peace for Philosophy

[416] Critical philosophy is the one that does not begin with an *attempt* to build or bolster systems, or even to support (as the moderatists do) a roof without a house for the purposes of occasional shelter; rather, it begins its conquest with the investigation of the *faculty* of human reason (whatever its intention may otherwise be), and does not ratiocinate into the blue heavens when discussion comes around to philosophemes that no possible experience could vouchsafe. Now, there is nevertheless in human reason something that cannot be known by any experience but that presents its reality and truth in effects demonstrated in experience and therefore can even be absolutely commanded (and indeed according to an a priori principle). This is the concept of freedom and the law of the categorical—i.e., absolutely commanding—imperative that descends from freedom. By way of this concept, *Ideas* that for merely speculative reason

would be completely empty, even though we were assigned them by reason itself as cognitive grounds of our final purpose, receive reality, albeit only a moral-practical reality: namely, to *comport* ourselves as if there were in fact the objects of these ideas (God and immortality), which one is therefore allowed to postulate from that (practical) point of view.

This philosophy, which is a perpetually armed state (against those who would perversely confuse appearances with things in themselves) and indeed an armed state that thereby also incessantly accompanies the activity of reason[4]—this philosophy opens the prospect of an eternal peace among philosophers by showing, on the one hand, the impotence of the *theoretical* proof of the opponent and by demonstrating, on the other, the strength of the *practical* reasons for the assumption of its principles. This peace has, in addition, the advantage of always keeping alert the powers of the subject exposed to the apparent danger of attacks, thereby promoting by means of philosophy the intention of nature to enliven the subject continually and to guard against the sleep of death [*Todesschlaf*].

* * *

Considered from this point of view, one must take the assertion of a man distinguished not only in his own field (mathematics) but [417] also in many others—a man rich in deeds who is adorned with a still flourishing old age—and interpret this assertion not as a message of misfortune but rather as a *felicitation,* when he completely denies philosophers the comfort of a peace that would let them rest on their supposed laurels.[3] For such a peace would only fatigue the

[3] If war is avoided forever,
If one follows what the wise one says,
Then all human beings maintain the peace,
The philosopher alone does not.

Kästner[c]

forces and would frustrate the purpose of nature with respect to philosophy, that is, a continual means of enlivening whose end is the final purpose of humanity; in contrast, a constitutional disposition toward conflict is not yet a war but, instead, should and can keep war at bay by a decisive preponderance of practical reasons over the contrary reasons, and it therefore should and can secure the peace.

B. Hyperphysical Foundation of the Life of Man on Behalf of a Philosophy of This Life

By means of reason, the human soul is endowed with spirit (*mens, nous*) so that man does not lead a *life* appropriate for a mere mechanism of nature and its technical-practical laws but also leads a life appropriate for the spontaneity of *freedom* and its moral-practical laws. This life-principle is not therefore based on concepts of the *sensible* objects, which all presuppose beforehand (prior to all practical use of reason) *science,* that is, theoretical knowledge; rather, this life-principle at first and immediately proceeds from an Idea of the *supersensible,* namely, *freedom,* and from the moral, categorical imperative, which makes us first aware of freedom, and it therefore justifies a philosophy whose doctrine is not (as in mathematics) a good instrument (tool for arbitrary ends), hence a mere means, but *duty in itself* making itself into its own principle.

What Is Philosophy, as a Doctrine [Lehre] *That Constitutes the Greatest Need of Man among All the Sciences?*

It is what its name already indicates: *the research of wisdom.* [418] Wisdom, however, is the harmony of the will with the *final purpose* (the highest good); and since this purpose, to the extent that it can be reached, is also a duty, and, conversely, to the extent that it is a duty, it also must be reachable, such a law of actions is called "moral." As a result, wisdom will be, for human beings, nothing other than the inner principle of the *will* to follow the moral law, whatever the *object* of the will may be. But this object will always be *supersensible,* because a will determined by an empirical object can very well justify a technical-practical observance of a rule but cannot ground any duty (which is a nonphysical relation).

On the Supersensible Objects of Our Knowledge

They are *God, freedom,* and *immortality.* (1) *God,* as the being that obligates all others; (2) *freedom,* as the faculty of man that allows him to maintain the observance of his duties (as though divine commands) against all the power of nature; (3) *immortality,* as a state in which good and ill will be imparted in relation to his moral worth.—One sees that they stand together, as it were, in the interconnection of the three propositions within an attributive *syllogism;* and since no objective reality can be given them from a theoretical point of view, precisely because they are Ideas of the supersensible, if one nevertheless wants to accord them such reality, it can be conceded to them that they have objective reality only from a practical point of view, as *postulates*[4] of moral-practical reason.

Among these Ideas, therefore, the middle one—namely, that of *freedom*—leads the other two in its train, since the existence of freedom is contained in the categorical imperative, which leaves no room for doubt, since this imperative, as the highest principle of wisdom and, consequently, as the one presupposing the final purpose of the most perfect will (the highest happiness in harmony with morality), [419] contains merely the conditions under which this final end

[4]A *postulate* is a practical imperative given a priori, capable of no explanation for its possibility (hence, also incapable of proof). One does not therefore postulate things or in general the *existence* of some object but only a maxim (rule) of action for a subject.—If it is a duty to bring into effect a certain purpose (the highest good), the *I* must also be entitled to assume that the conditions are there under which the performance of this duty is alone possible, although they are supersensible, and we (from a theoretical point of view) are capable of attaining no knowledge of them.[d]

can reach satisfaction. For the being that is alone able to accomplish this proportional distribution is God, and the state in which this accomplishment can be carried out among worldly beings endowed with reason—beings who alone are able to live up completely to this final purpose—consists in the assumption of a continuation of life already grounded in their nature, that is, *immortality.* For if the continuation of life were not therein grounded, it would mean only a *hope* for a future life but not a future life that reason necessarily has to presuppose (as a result of the moral imperative).

Result

It is therefore merely a misunderstanding—or a confusion of moral-practical principles of morality with theoretical principles, the first ones having the ability to yield *knowledge* with regard to the supersensible—if a conflict arises over what philosophy, as a doctrine of wisdom, says; and since there are no more objections of importance against this doctrine of wisdom and none can arise, one can with good reason

announce the near conclusion of a treaty for eternal peace in philosophy.

Second Part
Worrisome Prospect for a Near Eternal Peace in Philosophy

Mr. *Schlosser,* a man who has a great talent for writing and who has a mode of thought (there is reason to believe) that is attuned to the promotion of the good, ventured unexpectedly onto the battlefield of *metaphysics* so that he could recuperate, through leisurely activity, from an administration of the law under the conditions of authority and compulsion.[5] On this field disputes are carried out with far more bitterness than on the field he had just left. Critical philosophy, which he thinks he knows, although he has only looked at its latest results, and which he must necessarily have misunderstood because he did not go through the steps that lead to these results with careful diligence—this philosophy he finds revolting; and so he swiftly became a teacher "of a young man who (according to his account) wanted to study critical philosophy" in order to dissuade this student from critical philosophy without himself having previously taken any classes in it.

[420] His only advice is to clear away the *Critique of Pure Reason* wherever possible. This advice is like the assurance that good friends give to sheep: if they only want to get rid of dogs, live with them as brothers in constant peace.—If the student heeds this advice, he is then a toy in the hand of the master "to secure his taste (in Schlosser's own words) through writers of antiquity"[6] (in the art of persuasion by subjective reasons for approval, which takes the place of a method whereby conviction can be reached through objective reasons). Then he is sure: the student will let himself latch onto *the illusion of truth* (*verisimilitudo*) in the guise of *probability* (*probabilitas*), and latch onto the latter in judgments that can absolutely only proceed a priori from reason in the guise of certainty. "The coarse *barbaric* language of critical philosophy"[7] will not set him at ease, whereas it is, on the contrary, a *belletristic* expression dragged into the philosophy of the elements of human knowledge that must be seen as barbaric.—He deplores that "the wings should be clipped for all intimations, all perspectives on the supersensible, every genius of poetry"[8] (as if that were a concern of philosophy!).

The part of philosophy that contains *the theory of knowledge* (the theoretical part) and that, although directed for the most part toward limiting the exacting claims in theoretical knowledge, can under no condition be bypassed, sees itself compelled to go back to a *metaphysics* (of morals) as well as a complex of merely *formal* principles grounded in the concept of freedom before the question of purposes for action (the material of the will) can even be raised. Our anticritical philosophy leaps over this step, or he mistakes it so completely that he entirely misunderstands the principle that can serve as a touchstone for all *authorization: act in accordance with a maxim according to which you can at the same time will that it should be a universal law.* And he gives this principle a meaning that limits it to empirical conditions[9] and thus makes it unfit to be a canon of pure moral-practical reason (yet there must be one); he thereby throws himself into an entirely different field from the one toward which that canon points, and then he draws out adventuresome consequences.

But it is obvious that the issue here is not about a principle of employing a *means* to a certain *end* (for then it would be a pragmatic, [421] not a moral principle); at issue is not if the maxim of my will, once made into a universal law, contradicts the maxim of *someone else*'s will but, rather, if it contradicts *itself* (which I can judge a priori, according to the principle of contradictions, without any reference to experience, e.g., "Is equality of goods or property to be incorporated into my maxims?"); this contradiction is an unmistakable indication that the action is morally impossible. Mere ignorance, perhaps also some evil penchant for chicanery, could produce this attack, but it cannot, for all that, disrupt the

announcement of an eternal peace in philosophy.

For a peace treaty stipulating that, if only there is mutual understanding, each party is immediately (without capitulation) included in the treaty can also be, if not proclaimed as already concluded, then at least announced as near its conclusion.

* * *

If philosophy is represented simply as a *doctrine of wisdom* (which is also its literal meaning),[10] it cannot be overlooked as a theory of *knowledge* to the extent that this (theoretical) knowledge contains the elementary concepts employed by pure reason, granted that this knowledge only aims to demonstrate the boundaries of pure reason to reason itself. Now, it can hardly be expected of philosophy in the first sense to pose this question: whether one *should admit* freely and openly what one in fact knows of its object (sensible and supersensible) and whence this knowledge comes, or ask whether one only makes presuppositions from a practical point of view (because the assumption of this object helps to promote the final purpose of reason)?

It is possible that not everything a person holds to be true is *true* (for everyone can *err*), but in everything that one says, one must be *truthful* (one ought not to *deceive*); it may be that a confession is merely inward (before God) or also outward. The transgression of this duty of truthfulness is called *lying*, and, for this reason, there can be external as well as internal mendacity; as a result, it can happen that both sorts of mendacity are united or that they contradict each other.

But lying, whether it be inward or outward, is of two kinds: (1) if one states something to be *true* that one knows to be [422] untrue; (2) if one states something to be *certain* that one nevertheless knows to be subjectively uncertain.

Lying ("from the father of lies, through which all evil has come into the world"[11]) is the actual foul spot[12] on human nature, however much the tone of *truthfulness* (according to the example of many Chinese grocers who place above their shops an inscription in golden letters that reads "here one is never deceived") is the usual tone, above all, in matters that concern the supersensible.—The command *you ought not to lie* (even if it were done with the most pious intentions), inwardly incorporated as a principle into philosophy conceived as a doctrine of wisdom, would alone be able not only to bring about eternal peace in philosophy but also to secure it for all time to come.

Königsberg I. Kant

Notes on the Text

J. G. Schlosser reacted to Kant's "On a Newly Arisen Superior Tone in Philosophy" with a counterattack entitled "Letter to a young man who wanted to study critical philosophy" (*Schreiben an einen jungen Mann, der die kritische Philosophie studieren wollte* [Lübeck and Leipzig: F. Bohn, 1797]; the book actually appeared in 1796). In response to Kant's charge that certain aristocratic, and therefore exploitative, economic relations lie at the basis of his writing, Schlosser admits that his writing is based on only "liberal" labor (18), not on servility. He does not, however, respond to the accusation that his labor is exploitative; instead, he asserts that critical philosophy could be effective only in a time of "always growing monetary wealth. . . . However fantastic monetary wealth is, the inner worth of money is nil; its effect is nevertheless great" (7). Furthermore, Schlosser denies that he is a mystic and calls himself a "dogmatist" who draws the conclusion that the Bible is the word of God. This conclusion, he asserts, is more than reasonable, since—to cite only one example, but the one with which Schlosser is most concerned—it is highly improbable that "an almost metaphysical concept of divinity lay at the basis of the Israelite religion" (107) unless that concept were dictated by God himself. This version of Bishop Warburton's speculations on the "divine legation of Moses" leads Schlosser into a defense of probability, after which he concludes by noting that no Kantian could honestly accept an official position as a Christian teacher (122).

Kant's response, "Announcement of the Near Conclusion of a Treaty for Eternal Peace in Philosophy," first appeared in *Berlinische Monatsschrift* 28 (December 1796): 485–504. Schlosser, who was near death, took up this further challenge and wrote another counterattack, "Second letter to a young man who wanted to study critical philosophy, occasioned by the essay of Professor Kant on peace among philosophies" (*Zweites Schreiben an einen jungen Mann, der die kritische Philosophie studieren wollte, veranlasst durch den angehängten Aufsatz des Herrn Professor Kant über den Philosophienfrieden* [Lübeck and Leipzig: F. Bohn, 1798]). In this somewhat longer and very repetitive work, Schlosser concludes that he has been both misunderstood and ridiculed. After a protracted discussion of various classes of philosopher that, oddly enough, summarizes Kant's own system of classification, Schlosser asserts that Kant has not found a proper dietetic for thought but offered the "innoculation of an unhealthy sickness" (41). The "sickness" is religious skepticism. Above all, Kant's ethics is "inhuman" (65); his efforts to cut reason off from probabilities and analogies amount to an "emasculation" of human ethics (137). Since Kant severs human beings from senses and feelings, his philosophy cannot make people happier, truer, and better, but only more certain. Yet the only criterion of genuine philosophy, Schlosser asserts, is not certainty but improvement (139–40).

Kant did not react to Schlosser's renewed challenge. But others did. In a satirical essay entitled "The German Orpheus: The newest history of the Church," Friedrich Schlegel spared no term of abuse in his attack on Schlosser's philosophical talent (first published in *Deutschland,* 1796; reprinted in Schlegel, *Kritische Ausgabe,* eds. E. Behler, J. J. Anstett and H. Eichner [Munich: Schöningh, 1958], 8:3–10). Schlosser's *Schreiben* demonstrated "a model of common tone not to be surpassed" (4). "The most unbearable aspect," according to Schlegel, "is the self-congratulatory attitude with which he sets himself up against Kant as the representative of antiquity" (9), and the entire book is nothing but a "pastoral letter—for the fraternal fold of sheep who believe in mysticism" (10). Schlegel continued his attack on Schlosser with a review of his two books on Kant which was published in Fichte's *Philosophisches Journal* (1797). Schlegel almost repeats Kant, without the latter's "irony," when he opens the review with the statement that Schlosser "wants to *shine,* not to work" (33). Kant apparently read Schlegel's first review and was quite pleased (see Ernst Behler's introduction to Schlegel, *Kritische Ausgabe,* 8:cliv).

Friedrich Schiller was equally disturbed by Schlosser's writings and Schlegel's satirical response. After Goethe had sent him a copy of Schlosser's "Second Letter," Schiller would not restrain himself. Like Schlosser and Schlegel before him, Schiller cannot describe the dispute in which he has enlisted his energies without discovering a newly raised and deeply deceiving "tone": "Schlosser would have done better to have quietly swallowed the rebuke found in Kant's truth and in Friedrich Schlegel's impertinences. With his would-be apology he makes things worse for himself and leaves himself open in an unpardonable way. The book made me sick, I cannot deny it. . . . I found quite common salon chitchat clothed in an arrogant philosophical tone; he everywhere appealed to the common, lower interests of human nature, and never did I find a trace of an authentic interest in truth in itself. . . . And this affectation of such gentlemen to maintain man always in his totality, to spiritualize the physical and to humanize the spiritual, is, I fear, a lamentable effort to bring their poor selves out of anxious darkness and into the state of happiness" (letter to Goethe, 9 February 1798, *Schillers Werke,* ed. L. Blumenthal and B. von Wiese [Weimar: Böhlaus Nachfolger, 1943–77], 29:201–2). Goethe, who had earlier made a mild defense of Schlosser against Kant's charge that he was dishonest, was soon convinced that his brother-in-law's "Second Letter" was indeed mendacious; as he later wrote to Schiller, it gave ample evidence of "obstinacy, self-deception, and dishonesty" (10 February 1798, *Goethes Briefe,* ed. K. R. Mandelkow [Hamburg: Wegner, 1964], 2:328). During the controversy, Schiller addressed the following poem to Kant and included it among the *Xenien* collection (see *Schillers Werke,* 1:337):

An Kant

Vornehm nennst du den Ton der neuen Propheten? Ganz richtig,
Vornehm philosophiert heißt wie *Rotüre* gedacht.

(You call the tone of the new prophets superior? Entirely right,
Philosophizing in a superior way means thinking like a *commoner*).

The fullest and most incisive account of Schlosser's participation in a philosophical debate for which he was so obviously unprepared can be found in Friedrich Schelling's review of Schlosser's two books on Kant (first published in the *Jenaer Allgemeine Literatur-Zeitung* 299 [1798]; reprinted in F. W. J. von Schelling, *Sämtliche Werke,* ed. K. F. A. Schelling [Stuttgart and Augsburg: J. G. Cotta, 1856–61], 1:483–87). In his *Abhandlung zur Erläuterung des Idealismus der Wissenschaftslehre* (Treatise for the elucidation of the idealism of the theory of science), written in 1797, Schelling quotes from Kant's depiction of freedom as the Archimedean point on which philosophy rests ("On a Newly Arisen Superior Tone in Philosophy," 68 above) and uses this passage to defend the legitimacy of the conception of "intellectual intuition" which he and Fichte had developed (Schelling, *Sämtliche Werke,* 1:401). Like Schlosser, Schlegel and Schiller, Schelling takes over the terminology of *tone* and opens his treatise with an attack on those orthodox Kantians who believe that they can do without "all remaining culture" if only they repeat formulas drawn from the *Critiques* (see Schelling, *Sämtliche Werke,* 1:275–76).

Although Kant did not respond in writing to Schlosser's last attack, he is reported to have spoken conciliatory words not only of Schlosser but also of Count Stolberg. When Stolberg visited his publisher in Königsberg (Friedrich Nicolivius), he invited Kant to dinner, but Kant declined because, according to Stolberg, "he was afraid that I would find it unpleasant to see him" (see *Immanuel Kant in Rede und Gespräch,* ed. Rudolf Malter [Hamburg: Meiner, 1990], 434). Later, however, a meeting between the two was arranged, and Stolberg reported that Kant "spoke in an interesting way about meteorology, dreams, dietetic, and indeed about these things as a physiologist. He was natural and friendly. In short, I liked him" (435; Jachmann, Kant's friend and biographer, relates a somewhat different story). And in one of the most remarkable accounts of Kant's religious confession, the theologian Johann Friedrich Abegg relates a conversation that Johann Brahl once had with the aging Kant: "Brahl told me also: although he [Kant] postulates God, he himself does not believe in him, nor does he consider the future insofar as it can guarantee continuation [of the soul]. 'My God,' I said, 'to what, then, does he connect everything in morality other than God?'—'It is true,' Brahl said, 'in metaphysics he lets it remain undecided, does not react and does not desire. In morality, he is of the opinion that it really depends on the individual need, and in this respect he does not dispute Schlosser, who cannot live without a divine government. Kant, however, is completely independent'" (*Kant in Rede und Gespräch,* 445).

1. This paragraph is a variation on a theme from which Kant developed his conception of historical development. That conflict contributes to growth and therefore to the "health" of the human species at large indicates, according to the fourth proposition of the "Idea of Universal History from a Cosmopolitan Point of View," that nature is indeed wisely arranged (see Immanuel Kant, *Perpetual Peace and Other Essays,* trans. Ted Humphrey [Indianapolis, Ind.: Hackett Publishing Co., 1983], 31–32).

2. Schlosser is obviously the target of this remark. His response to Kant's essay was indeed a recommendation that "young men" not study critical philosophy lest they be emasculated (see Schlosser, *Schreiben,* 137).

3. See Cicero, *Tusculanes,* bk. 2, § 61: "Pompey related that Posidonius, as he lay in bed, discoursed weightily and fully on this very topic, that only the morally good is good. When fiery spasms of pain attacked him, he said repeatedly: 'You're wasting your time, pain. However troublesome you may be, I shall never admit that

you are an evil'" (Marcus Tullius Cicero, *Tusculan Disputations, II–V,* ed. and trans. A. E. Douglas [Warminster, England: Aris and Phillips, 1990], 53). See also Kant, *The Critique of Practical Reason,* trans. Lewis White Beck (Indianapolis, Ind.: Bobbs-Merrill, 1956), 62; 5:60.

4. Eternal peace in philosophy is therefore *not* like eternal peace among states organized into a world federation. For, according to the essay "Eternal Peace," it is the very fact that states find themselves in an "armed state" that inclines them and eventually impels them toward war. At the very beginning of the essay, Kant writes that "Standing armies (*miles perpetuus*) should be gradually abolished" (*Perpetual Peace,* 108; 8:345), and at the close of "On the Proverb: That May Be True in Theory, But Is of No Practical Use," he is even more graphic: "An enduring universal peace brought about by a so-called *balance of power in Europe* is a mere figment of imagination, like *Swift's house,* whose architect built it so perfectly in accord with all the laws of equilibrium that as soon as a sparrow lit on it, it fell in" (*Perpetual Peace,* 89; 8:312). In an essay principally devoted to an analysis of Hermann Cohen's *Deutschtum und Judentum* (1915), Derrida has written about this provision in the proposal for eternal peace; see the concluding remarks of Jacques Derrida, "Interpretations at War: Kant, the Jew, the German," *New Literary History* 22 (Winter 1991): 39–95.

5. Schlosser was in official service from 1773 to 1794, when he retired in order to write.

6. See Schlosser, *Schreiben,* 2.

7. See ibid., 6.

8. See ibid., 24.

9. See Schlosser's presentation of the categorical imperative as one that presupposes empirical knowledge of the entire system of nature; unless one had such knowledge, it would be impossible to legislate "universal laws" to nature (ibid., 47–48).

10. Kant may not have known Greek very well, but he knew quite well that the *eigentliche Bedeutung* of "philosophy" could not be *Weisheitslehre* ("doctrine of wisdom") unless *eigentlich* itself was no longer understood as "literal" but rather as something like "actual" or "authentic." But the very point of this paragraph is to indicate that such a definition is *not* the "actual" or "authentic" meaning of "philosophy" but is only its "literal" meaning. Its "actual" meaning lies in moral practice. How *philia* could so thoroughly drop out of the definition of "philosophy" when, according to the very opening lines of "On a Newly Arisen Superior Tone in Philos-

ophy" (see 51 above and Derrida's remarks, 126), the original error to which philosophy succumbs is an alteration in the meaning of its name constitutes a problem that Kant does not appear to be in a position to solve.

11. See John 8:44; Romans 5:12.

12. On the "foul spot" (*fauler Fleck*), see the more lengthy discussion in his book on religion: "This dishonesty [self-deception, mendacity with regard to the state of one's own conscience], by which we humbug ourselves and which thwarts the establishing of a true moral disposition in us, extends itself outwardly also to falsehood and deception. If this is not to be termed wickedness [*Bosheit*], it at least deserves the name of worthlessness, and is an element in the radical evil of human nature, which (inasmuch as it puts out of tune [*verstimmt*] the moral capacity to judge what a man is to be taken for, and renders wholly uncertain both internal and external attribution of responsibility) constitutes the foul taint in our race. So long as it is not eradicated, it prevents the seed of goodness from developing as it otherwise would" (Kant, *Religion within the Limits of Reason Alone,* trans. Theodore M. Greene and Hoyt H. Hudson [New York: Harper and Row, 1960], 33–34; 6:38).

Notes on the Footnotes

a. See Cicero, *De natura deorum,* bk. 2, § 64: "The pig has only one function—to supply us with food; Chrysippus, in fact, affirms that it was given a soul as a substitute for salt—to protect it from putrefaction" (Marcus Tullius Cicero, *Brutus, On the Nature of the Gods, On Divination, On Duties,* trans. Hubert M. Poteat [Chicago: University of Chicago Press, 1950], 289).

b. Kant often explored the significance and implications of the distinction between left and right. See the essay of 1768 which concerns the problem of incongruent counterparts, "On the First Foundation for the Distinction of Areas in Space" (2:377–83); the most extensive examination of this distinction is to be found in the 1786 essay "What Is Orientation in Thinking" (Kant, *Political Writings,* ed. Hans Reiss, trans. H. B. Nisbet [Cambridge: Cambridge University Press, 1990], 237–49).

c. The poem, which rhymes in the original, is entitled "On Eternal Peace." Abraham Gotthelf Kästner (1719–1800) was a famous mathematician and physicist in Göttingen, whom Kant called "the Nestor of all philosophical mathematicians in Germany" (13:278).

Heinrich Maier, editor of the Akademie edition, locates the poem Kant quotes in a posthumously published book of "poems and thoughts" (see 8:516). This volume was, of course, published after Kant's essay, and I have been unable to trace where Kant himself was able to read the poem. In the controversy with the Leibnizian philosopher J. A. Eberhard, Kästner had apparently taken the latter's side; in contrast to Kant's savage treatment of Eberhard, he paid great respect to Kästner's abilities as a mathematician and indeed tried to show that there was no essential difference between his conception of space and that of the mathematician (see Hans Saner, *Kant's Political Thought,* trans. E. B. Ashton [Chicago: University of Chicago Press, 1973], 148–51; cf. Henry E. Allison, *The Kant-Eberhard Controversy* [Baltimore: Johns Hopkins University Press, 1973], 12–13).

d. On postulates of pure practical reason, see the original discussion in the *Critique of Practical Reason,* 137–39; 5:132–34.

Other Exaltations

* * *

On Philosophical Exaltation[1]

6050.

[17:434] Plato correctly noted that we do not know things as they are in themselves through experience but, rather, learn to connect their appearances in a lawful manner. (He perceived, moreover, that knowledge of things according to the way they are in themselves also demands an intuition of things in themselves, that is, a purely intellectual intuition, which we are incapable of possessing.) He noted that in order for our representation to accord with the objective thing, it must be thought either to be produced by the object or as producing the object. The latter would be the original representation (*idea archetypa*), which is not within the capacity of human beings, if this representation is originally supposed to be in all its pieces. Therefore, the Ideas can be encountered only in the original being. But the Ideas of this original intellect cannot be concepts but only intuitions—indeed, intellectual ones. Now, he also believed that all knowledge a priori was knowledge of things in themselves,[2]

[1](The great difference between intellectual and empirical knowledge misled antiquity into exaltation.)

(Sects in China: I am the highest being.

Sects in Tibet: God is the gathering of everything sacred.)

[2][437] (And it is precisely the opposite. For there can only be synthetic a priori knowledge of things as appearances. For the form of sensibility with respect to intuition can be known prior to all objects, since it is given in the subject. Space and time. In this

and since we are participants in the former, we must also participate in the latter, and among the latter he counted mathematics. But we could not participate in mathematics from ourselves; consequently, we could do so only through the communication of divine Ideas. Since we must be conscious of these Ideas not as merely historically imparted and translated ones but, rather, as immediately perceived ones, they must not be implanted [435] concepts that are believed but rather immediate intuitions that we have from the archetypes in the divine intellect. But we can develop these archetypes only with much effort. They are therefore recollections of old Ideas from the community with God. Now, this is not yet exaltation but merely a way to explain the possibility of a priori knowledge. Yet at this point arises a presumption: participating now in this community with God and immediately intuiting these Ideas (mystical intuition) and indeed, finding in them the immediate object of all one's inclinations, which have hitherto turned toward appearances as types of such Ideas only out of a misunderstanding (mystical love of God). But since it is probable that there is between us and God a great ladder of creatures that stretches from us to him—astral spirits, aeons—one could first attain communion with these spirits and thus arrive at a prelude to intellectual, original appearances.[1] Since, however, the original Ideas are the cause of the reality of their

---

intuition, however, many synthetic propositions are given a priori, but are valid for nothing more, although its concepts as objects in general are merely intellectual, merely monograms that give nothing *in concrete* to knowledge but rather only knowledge *in abstracto*.)

(One obviously has analytic knowledge a priori, if the concept of the object is given, whether it be an empirical or a rational one. But synthetic a priori judgments would not be possible without pure intellectual intuition that is encountered only in God. What human beings are supposed to know synthetically and indeed a priori must have an object [*object*] of sensible intuition for its object [*zum Gegenstande*].)

objects, one could thereby hope to exercise dominion over nature, and so the Neo-Platonic school, which called itself eclectic in that they claimed to find their wisdom in everything ancient because they deceptively deposited all their dreamings into antiquity, were very accomplished in all the raving exaltation [*rasenden Schwärmerey*] with which they afflicted the world. (Finally Spinozism [Theosophy through intuition].) The Aristotelean philosophy repressed this delusion. One begins with concepts that we attain on the occasion of experience (*nihil est in intellectu*—). But one attained a priori knowledge without investigating how this is possible according to the highest principle. This philosophy was extended, and because everything that remains within the sensible world is always conditioned, reason drives the principles that are valid in this world ever higher and beyond sensibility itself, trusting that there will be just as secure an acquisition as had previously been available to explain objects at hand. The subjective conditions [436] of reason with respect to conceptualization now begin to be considered as objective conditions of things in themselves, and, since reason is not satisfied until it comprehends the whole, the supersensible world begins to be conquered. Because there are no limits to explain where one could stop, one must finally remove the separate existence of all things, since the possibility of individual and isolated existing was taken from them, and must bequeath to them only the inherence in a subject. Spinozism is the true conclusion to dogmatic metaphysics. Critique of propositions has no success here. For the difference between the subjective and the objective with respect to their validity cannot be recalled, because the subjective propositions that are at the same time objective have not been previously distinguished. The necessity of assuming them is at once there, and one does not notice that they are merely subjective. Nobody hits upon the notion that experience is possible merely on the basis of a priori principles. Only a critique of reason itself can manage to do anything here. In the meantime, men still hold back for a while the fall into exaltation by luminous reason surveying the vast expanse of both used and misused opinions.—If one does not want to break open the way of critique, one must let exaltation go its own way and laugh about it with Shaftesbury.[2]

6051.

The origin of all philosophical exaltation lies in Plato's original divine intuitions of all possible objects,[3] that is, of the Ideas, since we have only an intuition of them through their appearances, therefore only passively. On this is based, first of all, Plato's opinion that all our a priori knowledge (mathematics), especially the knowledge of perfections, stems from the recollection of these onetime intuitions, and we must forever afterward seek to develop them; but from here emerges the second step of mysticism, to have an intuition of everything now in God, which thus makes all research into synthetic a priori knowledge unnecessary in that we read this knowledge in God [*indem wir sie in Gott lesen*]. Third step: since other beings may be closer to God, we, so to speak, must first get to know those [438] Ideas perhaps through reflection; consequently, we must associate with spiritual natures.

[3](Even before Plato, one distinguished intellectual from empirical knowledge and understood the latter, which one called "sensible," and thus one made an absolute difference between intelligible and sensible things. One considered all a priori knowledge to be intellectual, therefore also mathematics; and since many different things can be known by the senses and only the latter in fact a priori, one had examples of presumably intellectual knowledge. But in order to find this difference important, reason had to have a need [*Bedürfnis*] to go beyond the empirical, because the empirical is always conditioned and so can never be the thing in itself, which must always have the completion of its conditions.

One considered the necessity of the hypothesis of such a thing to be an insight into the necessity of this thing.)

The highest level of exaltation is that we ourselves are in God and feel or intuit in him our existence. The second highest: that we have an intuition of all things according to their true nature only in God as their cause and in his Ideas as archetypes. The third: that we do not have an intuition of them at all, but they nevertheless derive from the concept of God and therefore allow for an inference from our existence and our rational concepts of things directly to the existence of God in whom they alone can have objective reality. Now back from the lowest level to the highest: Spinoza.

6052.

The cause of exaltation is the lack of a critique of reason itself. For if I attain from my own powers the derivation of all things from a One and also attain the qualities of this One, how did I get so far? (1) By analyzing my concepts? Then, the concepts have been inspired [*inspirit*] into me originally. (2) By the synthesis of laws of experience? But then I remain in the world. (3) By principles that I take from neither of these two? This must then be a secret intuition of the supersensible.

6053.

Superstitious religion bases itself on a principle of subjecting reason to the delusion of perceptions.

In exaltation human beings raise themselves above humanity.

On a Newly Raging Spirit of Domination in Philosophy

[23:195] *Schiller*[3]

On a newly raging spirit [*Geist*] of domination in philosophy.

That everyone holds an opinion that he publicly confesses as worthy of being universally dominant [*herrschend*] already lies in the concept of opinion itself and completely accords with the freedom to think according to the rule of *audiatur et altera pars* [the other side should also be heard]; that is, not to be *beyond* the reason of others but, rather, to be *by its means* a co-proprieter (*condominus*) of the great store of knowledge that universal human reason offers as a possession and indeed not a co-proprieter who simply uses this property (*dominus vtile*) and then only, as it were, as a fiefdom (*dominium vtile*) but rather as a co-proprieter who, being the fundamental proprieter, immediately (as *dominus directus*) has it at his disposal. The slogan of this employment of reason, which is limited by no preferential right of one despotically peremptory authority over the opinion of another, is contained in the sentence: *audiatur et altera pars.* And even if a voice supposedly heard from heaven were to contradict the voice of human reason, then everyone must freely be able to doubt that it is such a heavenly voice after all.—Now a certain spirit of domination (of presumed preference and privilege) has recently been raging: a spirit of domination over the free and public use of merely theoretical reason which threatens to cut off not only thinking out loud but also does so in order not to think (in a certain way and, in this way, to confiscate reason).

There are two fields in which pure reason tries to acquire a possession, mathematics and philosophy.—In the first case no one has ever claimed an ability to decide over it on the basis of authority, but this claim can do no harm, since mathematics is merely an instrument, whereas philosophy alone can determine the final purpose of human reason and with mere concepts of reason de- [the text breaks off here].

On Exaltation and the Remedy for It

[11:138] You ask me where the tendency to the now so prevailing exaltation comes from, and how we could be cured of this evil?[4] Both questions are tasks as difficult to solve for physicians of the soul [*Seelenärtze*] as the so-called Russian catarrh (influenza) was for our physicians of the body—a disease that a few years ago suddenly made its course around the world, struck many unchecked and then stopped by itself. Physicians of the body have something in common with those of the soul: they describe the sicknesses better than they can understand their origin or can cure them; it is lucky for the ill patients if their doctors' prescriptions are only dietary and if they simply recommend pure, cold water as a remedy, letting good nature do the rest.

As I see it, the universally disseminated *mania for reading* [Lesesucht] not [139] only is the guiding instrument (vehicle) in the spread of this disease but also is the poison (miasma) that engenders it. Those who are well-to-do, including the superior caste [*vornehmere Stand*], who, at the very least claim equality in their insights with—if they do not actually claim superiority over—those who must exert effort on the thorny path of thorough learning, are content to skim, as it were, the cream of the sciences in compendia and in summarizing excerpts. But they want to wipe away the inequality that soon strikes you in the eye between an honest ignorance and thorough science, and this succeeds best when someone takes aim at incomprehensible things as facts [*Facta*] that can only be thought as a pleasant possibility, and one then demands that the well-grounded and thorough natural scientist give an explanation: how would such a scientist explain, for instance, the fulfillment of this or that dream, this intimation, astrological prediction, or transformation of lead into gold, and so forth. If the fact is admitted (which he does not want to contest), then one person is just as ignorant as the other. It was too difficult for him to learn *everything* and to know what the scientist knows; therefore, he seeks an easier way to make the inequality disappear by bringing things into a path about which neither of them can know anything and in which neither can have any insight; he therefore has the freedom to make any sort of judgment he wants about things in which neither he nor the scientist can do any better.—From there the mania spreads out also into the community.

Against this evil, I see no other remedy than to pull back from the teaching of many and widely varied things [*Vielerleilernen*] in the schools and to reintroduce the thorough teaching of a few things. This is not so much to eliminate the desire for reading as to give it a direction so that it becomes intentional and has a point; in this way, the well-instructed ones are pleased with only those things they have read that procure them a real acquisition of insight, whereas everything else makes them sick.—A German doctor (Mr. Grimm[5]), as a traveler, has made a remark about *French all-knowingness,* as he calls it. But this is not so tasteless as what takes place when a German makes a solid and secure system that he does not easily abandon, whereas a *mesmerist* in France is only a fashionable item and soon thereafter entirely disappears.

This is the usual trick of the trade whereby the exalting ones give their ignorance the veneer of [140] science: they ask, do you know the true cause of the magnetic force, or do you know the matter that produces such wonderful effects in electrical phenomena? Now, they believe they can discuss with good grounds something of whose inner constitution, in their opinion, the greatest natural scientists know as little as they do, even with respect to its most likely effects. But the natural scientist considers valid only those effects that he can place before his eyes in an experiment, by means of which he brings them entirely within his power, whereas the exalting ones snatch up effects that could originate from both the observing person and the observed person and cannot therefore be subject to a true experiment.

Against these shenanigans there is nothing to do but magnetize the animal magnetizers and grant space for disorganization, so long as it pleases them and others who are easily fooled; there is nothing more to do but to recommend to the police that morality not be too closely trodden upon, and, for the rest, to follow the only path of research into nature, through the experimentation and observation that lets us become familiar with the properties of objects of the outer senses. A wide-ranging refutation is against the dignity of reason, and it does nothing to straighten out the situation; contemptuous silence is more fitting for such insanity, as when similar events in the moral world last for a short time in order to make room for other kinds of foolishness.[6]

Preface to Reinhold Bernhard Jachmann's "Testing of Kantian Religious Philosophy"

Prospectus for the Enclosed Work

[8:441] *Philosophy,* as a theory [*Lehre*] of science, like every other doctrine [*Doktrin*], can be used as a tool for every sort of purpose, but it has in this respect only a *conditioned* value.[7] Whoever intends to make this or that product must get to work in this or that way, and if one proceeds according to *principles,* then these principles can also be called a *practical* philosophy and have a value, like every commodity and all labor, insofar as it is able to enter into commercial traffic.

But philosophy in the literal meaning of the word, as a doctrine of wisdom [*Weisheitslehre*], has an *unconditioned* value. For it is the doctrine of the *final purpose* of human nature, which can only be a unique end to which all other ends mut be held inferior or be subordinated, and the perfected *practical* philosophy (an ideal) is the one that fulfills in itself this demand.

Whether wisdom is *poured into* men from above (through inspiration) or *climbs up* from below by the inner power of practical reason—that is the question.

The one who maintains inspiration as a passive means to obtain knowledge conceives a monstrosity [*Unding*]: the possibility of *supersensible experience,* which is a complete contradiction in itself (the transcendent represented as immanent). And he bases himself on a secret doctrine called mysticism, which is the exact opposite of philosophy, and yet precisely because it (like alchemy), being in possession of the grand discovery, is superior to all the work of rational yet painful research into nature, it blissfully dreams in the sweet state of pleasure.

The author of the present work, my former diligent and animated auditor, now very esteemed friend, has tried in this writing with great success to eradicate this pseudophilosophy, or he has attempted, rather, not to let it rise up wherever it stirs. The book does not at all need my recommendation, but I would only like to attach the seal of friendship on this book for the author with everlasting remembrance.

Königsberg I. Kant

14 January 1800

Notes on the Text

"On Philosophical Exaltation" is a draft that, according to the editors of the Akademie edition, was written sometime during the 1780s; the boldface numbers refer to the ordering of Kant's papers. These brief texts amplify the "nonliterary" interpretation of Plato that Kant had first proposed in the section of the *Critique of Pure Reason* on "Ideas in General" (A 312–20; B 368–77). Since they contain numerous references to Spinoza, it is not unlikely that they were intended for Kant's much requested contribution to the "conflict over pantheism" that was ignited by Friedrich Jacobi's assertion that Lessing had, near the end of his life, admitted that he was a follower of Spinoza. The most thorough discussion of this conflict in English is to be found in Frederick Beiser, *The Fate of Reason* (Cambridge, Mass.: Harvard University Press, 1987), 92–108.

"On a Newly Raging Spirit of Domination in Philosophy" is most likely a draft of "On a Newly Arisen Superior Tone in Philosophy" and was therefore written sometime before 1796. It is not clear, however, that Schlosser is the target, since the first line is "Schiller." If it was, indeed, Friedrich Schiller who was supposed to be the polemical object of the essay, it may have been written in response to Kant's reading of "On Grace and Dignity" (first published in *Neue Thalia,* vol. 3, 1793), and was then perhaps written before Schiller's request that Kant contribute something to his new journal, *Die Horen* (see Kant's letter of 30 March 1795 in Kant, *Philosophical Correspondence,* ed. and trans. Arnulf Zweig [Chicago: University of Chicago Press, 1967], 221–22; 12:10–11). See my note 3 below for a brief discussion of who "Schiller" might be and why his name appears at the top of the page.

"On Exaltation and the Remedy for It" is a letter Kant wrote to his longtime friend L. Ernst Borowski (1740–1832), who has since become famous for his striking presentation of Kant's daily life. In 1790, Borowski wrote a pamphlet called *Cagliostro, einer der merkwürdigsten Abentheuer unsres Jahrhundert. Seine Geschichte nebts Raisonnement über ihn und den schwärmerischen Unfug unsrer Zeit überhaupt* (Königsberg: F. Nicolivius, 1790). Borowski thanked Kant for his "*powerful* words against this thing, exaltation" (11:142), and he appended Kant's letter to the future editions of his pamphlet, perhaps with tacit permission. It has been reprinted in various editions of Kant's work under the above title, although the Akademie editors include it among the letters (11:138–40). It has been dated "between 6 and 22 March 1790." It has been previously translated by Arnulf Zweig in his edition of Kant's *Philosophical Correspondence,* 159–61.

Of the writings in this section, only the "Preface to Reinhold Bernhard Jachmann's *Testing of Kantian Religious Philosophy*" was published by Kant. It was, as it were, his last word of philosophy, and it is once again a clarification of the meaning of the word *philosophy.* Kant's brief text served as the preface to Jachmann, *Prüfung der Kantischen Religionsphilosophie in Hinsicht auf die ihr beygelegte Aehnlichkeit mit dem reinen Mystizism* [Testing of Kant's philosophy of religion with respect to the similarity to pure mysticism that has been attributed to it] (Königsberg: F. Nicolovius, 1800). Jachmann's book is a response to the "similarity" discovered by Carol Arnold Willmans, *De similitudine inter Mysticismum purum et Kantianum religionis doctrinam* (Halle: Bielefelda-Guestphalo, 1797). In the appendix to the first part of the *Conflict of Faculties* on the "conflict" with the faculty of theology, Kant prints a letter that Willmans had sent him concerning "a pure mysticism in religion" (see *The Conflict of the Faculties,* 7:69–75).

1. It is remarkable that Kant does not mention Swedenborg here, since he was the object of Kant's most lengthy and perhaps most famous attack on the notion of disembodied spirits; see Kant,

Dreams of a Spirit-Seer, trans. John Manolesco (New York: Vantage Press, 1969). After the publication of the first *Critique,* Kant's polemics against *Schwärmerei* cease to be so closely bound up with attempts to explain the phenomenon through recourse to physiology; instead, Kant almost always returns to the history of philosophy and thus alters the basis of explanation from biological causality to historical and genealogical nexes.

2. The reference is to Anthony Ashley Cooper, third earl of Shaftesbury, "A Letter on Enthusiasm," *Characteristics of Men, Manners, Opinions, Times* (1711, reprint, Gloucester, Mass.: Peter Smith, 1963).

3. The editors of the Akademie edition suspect that Kant simply mistook Schiller for Schlosser (a mistake that would doubtless have horrified Schiller, especially when one considers his own very hostile reaction to Schlosser's writings). But it is not altogether impossible that when Kant wrote and underlined *Schiller,* he meant no one else *but* Schiller. For Schiller is not so different from Schlosser, at least from the perspective of Kant's refutation of their respective positions. Both wish to rescue "inclinations" and "feeling" from their humiliation in the face of pure practical reason; both are afraid of a certain "emasculation" of sensibility to which Kant's conception of morality exposes the fully developed human being. In his response to Schiller's "On Grace and Dignity," Kant finds the same procedure at work in Schiller that he will later discover in Schlosser: "inclinations" are raised (and thus cease to be *inclined*), while reason at the same time condescends to meet inclinations at a balanced midpoint, the precise point of grace. Every *graceful* elevation is done, however, *without work.* So Kant recommends that both Schiller and Schlosser reconsider their relation to labor; it is hardly an accident that Kant refers to Hercules' arduous labors in his respectful response to Schiller in the same spirit in which he will later refer to these labors in his lampooning of Schlosser: "Professor Schiller, in his masterly treatise (*Thalia,* 1793, pt. 3) on *grace* and *dignity* in morality, objects to this [rigoristic] way of representing obligation, as carrying with it a monastic cast of mind. . . . Only after vanquishing monsters did Hercules become Musagetes, leader of the muses,—after labors from which those worthy sisters, trembling, drew back" (Kant *Religion within the Limits of Reason Alone,* trans. Theodore M. Greene and Hoyt H. Hudson [New York: Harper and Row, 1960], 18–19; 6:23). Although it is difficult to understand why Kant would attack Schiller in matters of "property," his concern in both this fragment and the footnote to the

Religion is with the character of an authoritative voice whose origin seems to be that of heaven. Yet it is *also* possible that Kant simply placed the name Schiller on the top of the draft for entirely extraneous reasons; it was perhaps a reminder to write to Schiller about his request for a contribution to *Die Horen* and had nothing at all to do with the text that follows. (I thank Eckart Förster for a very helpful discussion about Kant's writing habits in his later years.)

4. The "evil" was the spread of Cagliostro's influence, mesmerism, and the practice of hypnosis. The basis of this "disease" was the establishment of "societies of harmony" throughout Europe.

5. See J. F. C. Grimm, *Bemerkungen eines Reisenden durch Deutschland, Frankreich, England und Holland* (Altenburg: Richter, 1775).

6. Kant will later call this tendency of the "moral world" to pass from one version of "insanity" to another *Abderitism* (perhaps named in honor of Martin Christoph Wieland's extraordinary novel, *Geschichte der Abderiten*). Much of the second section of *The Conflict of the Faculties* is devoted to showing why the "Abderitian hypothesis"—the hypothesis, namely, that the world is so completely dominated by "insanity" that it neither progresses nor regresses but only moves in place—can be refuted once and for all (see 7:82).

7. The opening sentence of an earlier version of this preface is more explicit: "Philosophy (in the particular meaning of the word) as doctrine of wisdom [*Weisheitslehre*], that is, as a science of the final purpose of human reason, is the exact opposite [*Widerspiel*] of the philosophy that one places under the title of mysticism" (23:467). This version of the preface is far more polemical against mysticism and its *lapis philosophorum* than the version Kant published, but it is not clear who the object of his attack might have been.

Derrida

On a Newly Arisen Apocalyptic Tone in Philosophy

* * *

I shall speak then of/in an apocalyptic tone in philosophy.

The Seventy have bequeathed us a translation of *gala.* It is called the Apocalypse.

In Greek, *apokalupsis* would translate words derived from the Hebrew verb *gala.* I am referring here, without drawing any authority from them, to some indications of André Chouraqui to which I shall return. But I must forewarn you right now: the (hi)stories or enigmas of translation that I hear spoken of, that I intend to speak about, and that I shall get myself entangled in for reasons more serious than my incompetence, they are, I believe, without solution or exit.

That will be my theme. More than a theme, a task (*Aufgabe des Übersetzers,* Benjamin's just assignation) I shall not discharge.

The other day Jean Ricardou asked me—we were talking then about translation—to say a little more about what I had sketched out on a grace given beyond work, thanks to [*grâce au*] work, but without it. I was talking then of a *gift* "given there" ("*il y a,*" *es gibt*), but above all given there without having, *in the final account,* to be merited in responsibility. One must translate and one must not translate. I am thinking of the *double bind* of YHWH when, with the name of his choice, with his own name one could say, Babel, he gives *to translate and not to translate.* And no one, forever, since then, eludes the double postulation.

Well, to Jean Ricardou I shall reply as follows and do so

in the form of an elliptical thanks for what I am given here, given to think or simply given, beyond the thinkable, that is to say—that would be to say in German—beyond all memory and some thanks, given by our hosts at Cerisy, by Philippe Lacoue-Labarthe and by Jean-Luc Nancy, by all you with so much work and grace, so much grace in your work: translation-proof, grace would perhaps come when the writing of the other absolves you, from time to time, from the infinite *double bind* and first of all—such is the gift's condition—absolves itself, unbinds itself from this double bind, unburdens or clears itself, it, the language [*langue*] of writing, this given trace that always comes from the other, even if it is no one. To clear oneself of the gift, of the given gift, of giving itself, is the grace that I now know you have and in any case that I wish for you. This grace is always improbable; it is never proved. But must we not believe it happens? That was perhaps, yesterday, belief itself. Another way of saying: for what you have given me during these ten days I not only thank you, I pardon you. But who can authorize him- or herself to pardon? Let's say that I ask pardon for you, of you yourselves for you yourselves.

Apokaluptō no doubt was a good word [*bon mot*] for *gala. Apokaluptō,* I disclose, I uncover, I unveil, I reveal the thing that can be a part of the body, the head or the eyes, a secret part, the sex or whatever might be hidden, a secret, the thing to be dissimulated, a thing that is neither shown nor said, signified perhaps but that cannot or *must* not first be delivered up to self-evidence. *Apokekalummenoi logoi* are indecent remarks. So it is a matter of the secret and the *pudenda.*

The Greek tongue shows itself hospitable here to the Hebrew *gala.* As André Chouraqui recalls in his short "Limiaire pour l'Apocalypse" of John (of which he recently offered a new translation),[1] the word *gala* recurs more than

[1]Translation from the Greek, of course, but with some conditions I must specify here, at once because they will be in question in the

one hundred times in the Hebrew Bible and seems in effect to say *apokalupsis,* disclosure, uncovering, unveiling, the veil lifted from about the thing: first of all, if we can say this, man's or woman's sex, but also their eyes or ears. Chouraqui specifies:

---

course of the discussion and because what is at stake could be named the *appropriation* of apocalypse: that is also the theme of this exposition. In sum, Chouraqui's very singular attempt consists, for John's Apocalypse as well as for the New Testament generally, in reconstituting a new Hebrew original, under the Greek text at our disposal, and *in acting as if* he were translating that *phantom* original text about which he supposes that, linguistically and culturally, it had already had to let itself be translated (if that can be said in a largely metaphorical sense) in the so-called original Greek version. "The translation I publish, nourished by the contribution of the traditional versions, has the calling to search under the Greek text for its historical context and its Semitic substratum. Such a course [*démarche*] is possible today" (*Un Pacte neuf: Lettres, Contemplation de Yohanân,* trans. André Chouraqui [Paris: Desclée de Brouwer, 1977], 9). According to Chouraqui, it passes through an "Aramaic or Hebrew retroversion" of the Greek text taken for a "filter." So the historic translations of the New Testament into Aramaic or Hebrew will have played here an indispensable but only a mediating role.

> Even if the text is expressed in Greek and, for what is from Jesus, if it is based on an Aramaic or a Hebrew (Mishnaic, rabbinic, or Qumranic) whose traces have disappeared, the thought of the Evangelists and the Apostles has as ultimate terms of reference the word of YHWH, that is, for all of them, the Bible. It is the Bible that is recovered in analyzing the Greek text, even if one must preliminarily pass through an Aramaic filter or through that of the translation of the Seventy. . . .
>
> . . . Starting from the Greek text, knowing the techniques of the translations from the Hebrew into Greek, and the Hebrew resonances of the Koine, I have tried with each word, with each verse, to touch the Semitic ground in order then to return to the Greek that it was necessary to recover, enriched by

> Someone's ear is uncovered in lifting up the hair or the veil that covers it in order to whisper a secret into it, a word [*parole*] as hidden as a person's genitals. YHWH can be the agent of this disclosure, this uncovering. The arm or the glory of YHWH can also be uncovered to man's gaze or ear. So nowhere does the word *apocalypse* [concludes the translator referring here as well to the Greek as to the Hebrew] have the sense it finally takes on in French and other tongues: fearsome catastrophe. Thus the Apocalypse is essentially a contemplation (*hazôn*) [and in fact Chouraqui translates what we are accustomed to call the Apocalypse of John by *Contemplation of Yohanân*] or an inspiration [*neboua*] at the sight, the uncovering or disclosure of YHWH and, here, of Yéshoua' the Messiah. [*Un Pacte neuf*, 157]

Perhaps it would be necessary, and I thought for a moment of doing this, to collect [*lever*] or bring out [*relever*] all the senses pressing around this Hebrew *gala,* vis-à-vis the columns and colossi of Greece, vis-à-vis the galactic under all the *voies lactées,* the *milky ways* whose constellation had not long ago fascinated me. Curiously, there again we would have found significations like those of stone [*pierre*], of stone rolls, of cylinder, of parchment rolls and books, of rolls that envelop or furnish, but above all (and this is what I retain for the moment) the idea of laying bare [*mise à nu*], of spe-

---

> a new substance, before passing to the French. [*Un Pacte neuf,* 11–12]

Such is the project; it gives as its reference a *double authority* and invokes in turn the "quasi-unanimity of the exegetes" or "the great ecumenical current," the "ecumenism of sources" [11, 15, 16]. For multiple reasons I shall not discuss directly the authority of these authorities. But when the matter concerns language, text, event, and destination, etcetera, the questions I shall propose today could not have been unfolded if the foundation of such authorities had to be kept under cover in the unquestionable. A secondary consequence of this precaution: it is not as to an *authorized* translation that I shall often refer to that of André Chouraqui.

cifically apocalyptic unveiling, of the disclosure that lets be seen what until then remained enveloped, withdrawn, held back, reserved, for example, the body when the clothes are removed or the glans when the foreskin is removed in circumcision. And what seems the most remarkable in all the biblical examples I was able to find and must forgo exposing here is that the gesture of denuding or of affording sight [*donner à voir*]—the *apocalyptic* movement—is more serious here, sometimes more culpable and more dangerous than what follows and what it can give rise to, for example, copulation. Thus when, in Genesis 9:21, Noah gets drunk and uncovers himself in his tent, Ham sees his father's genitals, and his two brothers to whom he reports this come to cover Noah again but turn away from him in order not to see his sex. Even there the unveiling is not the most culpable moment of a copulation. But when YHWH, speaking to Moses, declares a certain number of sexual prohibitions, the fault does indeed seem to consist essentially in the unveiling that affords seeing. Thus, in Leviticus 20:11, 17:

> The man who lies with his father's wife
> has uncovered his father's sex.
> Both are put to death . . . .
> . . . .
> The man who takes his sister,
> his father's daughter or his mother's daughter,
> he sees her sex,
> she sees his sex:
> it is incest.[1]

But the terrifying and sacred gravity of this apocalyptic uncovering is not any the less, of course, in the case of the arm of YHWH, of his glory, or of ears open to his revelation. And the disclosure not only opens to vision or contemplation, affords not only seeing but also hearing/understanding.

For the moment I forgo interpreting all the accords between *gala* and the *apocalyptic,* the Hebrew and the Greek. These accords are numerous and powerful; they support—even if they do not exclude dissonances, deviations, or betrayals—the great concert of translations.

In order to let them resound all alone, I have chosen to speak to you rather of/in an apocalyptic tone newly adopted in philosophy. No doubt I wanted thus to mime in citation but also to transform into a genre, and then parody, deport, deform the well-known title of a perhaps less well-known pamphlet of Kant, *Von einem neuerdings erhobenen vornehmen Ton in der Philosophie* (1796). The established French translation: *D'un ton grand seigneur adopté naguère en philosophie.* The English translation: "On a Newly Arisen Superior Tone in Philosophy."[2] What happens to a title when made to undergo this treatment? when it begins thus to resemble the category of a genre, here a genre that comes down to mocking those who give themselves a genre?

In making this choice, I also hoped to go meet those who, in one of the seminars of these ten days, have precisely organized their work by privileging the reference to a certain Kantian caesura in the time of philosophy.

But I also let myself be seduced by something else. The attention to tone, which is not just style, seems rather rare to me. Tone has been little studied for itself, if we suppose that is possible or has ever been done. A tone's distinctive signs are difficult to isolate, if they even exist in complete purity, which I doubt, above all in a written discourse. By what is a tone marked: a change or a rupture of tone? And how do you recognize a tonal difference within the same corpus? What traits are to be trusted for analyzing this, what signposting [*signalisation*] neither stylistic, nor rhetorical, nor evidently thematic or semantic? The extreme difficulty of this question, indeed of this task, becomes more accentuated in the case of philosophy. Isn't the dream or the ideal of philosophical discourse, of philosophical address [*allocution*], and of the writing supposed to represent that address, isn't it to make tonal difference inaudible, and with it a whole desire, affect, or scene that works (over) the concept in contraband? Through what is called neutrality of tone, philosophical discourse must also guarantee the neutrality or at least the imperturbable serenity that should accompany the relation to the true and the universal. Consequently, will it be possible to listen to or detect the tone of a philosopher, or rather (this precision is important) the so-called or would-be philosopher?

And if someone promised us to do this, wouldn't that person be engaging to pick out all the traits that in a corpus are not yet or no longer philosophical, all the regrettable deviations in relation to the atonal norm of philosophical address?

In fact, if Kant did have the audacity, very singular in history, to concern himself systematically with a certain tone in philosophy, we must immediately nuance the praise we would like to give him for this. First, it is not certain that he is bent on or succeeds in analyzing the pure phenomenon of a tonality, as we are going to verify. Next, less does he analyze a tone in philosophy than denounce a *manner* of giving oneself airs; now it is a manner or a mannerism that, precisely, does not seem to him to be a very good tone [*de très bon ton;* also, in very good taste] in philosophy and so marks already a deviation in relation to the norm of philosophical discourse. More seriously, he attacks a tone that announces something like *the death of philosophy.*

The expression is Kant's and appears twice in this twenty-page lampoon; each time, this death is associated with the idea of a supernatural revelation, of a vision provoking a mystic exaltation or at least a visionary's pose. The first time, it is a question of a "supernatural communication" or a "mystical illumination" ("*übernatürliche Mitteilung, mystische Erleuchtung*") that promises a substitute or a supplement, a surrogate of a knowable object, "which is then the death of all philosophy (*der Tod aller Philosophie*)" [8:398]. And right near the end, Kant warns against the danger of an "exalting vision (*schwärmerische Vision*), which is the death of all philosophy" (once more "*der Tod aller Philosophie*") [8:405].

Kant's comments are also marked with the tone he gives himself, with the effects he searches for, with his polemical or satiric verse. This is a social critique, and its premises have a properly political character. But if he derides a tone that announces the death of all philosophy, the tone in itself is not what is being mocked. Besides, the tone itself—what is it? Is it something other than a distinction, a tonal difference that no longer refers except by figure to a social code, to group or caste mores, to class behaviors, by a great number of relays that no longer have anything to do with the pitch [*la hauteur*] of the voice or of the timbre? Although, as I suggested a moment ago, the tonal difference does not pass for the essentially philosophical, the fact that there is tone, tonal marking, is not by itself alone, for Kant, what announces the death of all philosophy. It is a certain tone, a certain inflection socially coded to say such and such a determinate thing. The tonal loftiness [*la hauteur*] he overwhelms with his sarcasm remains a metaphoric loftiness. These people speak in a lofty pitch [or loudly]; these loudspeakers raise the voice, but this is said only by figure and by reference to social signs. Kant never disregards [*fait abstraction de*] the content. Nevertheless—this fact is far from insignificant—the first time a philosopher comes to speak of the tone of other self-styled philosophers, when he comes to inaugurate this theme and names it in his very title, it is in order to be frightened or indignant faced with the death of philosophy. He brings to judgment those who, by the tone they take and the air they give themselves when saying certain things, place philosophy in danger of death and tell philosophy or philosophers the imminence of their end. The imminence matters no less than the end. The end is near, they seem to say, which does not exclude that it may have already taken place, a little as in John's Apocalypse the imminence of the end or of the last judgment does not exclude a certain " ' "you are dead. / Stay awake!" ' " [3:1–2], whose dictation follows close on the allusion to a " 'second death' " that will never overtake the victor.

Kant is sure that those who speak in this tone expect some benefit from it, and that is what will first interest me.

What benefit? What bonus of seduction or intimidation? What social or political advantage? Do they want to cause fear? Do they want to give pleasure? To whom and how? Do they want to terrify? To blackmail? [*Faire chanter?*] To lure into an outmatching in enjoyment? Is this contradictory? In view of what interests, *to what ends* do they wish to come with these heated proclamations on the end to come or the end already accomplished? I wanted to speak to you today a little about this: in/of a certain tone and of what comes [*arrive*] to philosophy as its death, of the relation between this tone, this death, and the apparently calculated benefit of this eschatological mystagogy. The eschatological tells the *eskhaton,* the end, or rather the extreme, the limit, the term, the last, what comes *in extremis* to close a history, a genealogy, or very simply a countable series.

Mystagogues, that is Kant's word and specific charge. Before coming to my topic [*propos*], I shall draw out some paradigmatic traits in Kant's indictment, paradigmatic and contraparadigmatic traits, for I am perhaps, in repeating what he does, going to come round to doing the contrary—or preferably something else.

The mystagogues make a scene; that is what interests Kant. But at what moment do the mystagogues come on the scene and sometimes go into a trance? At what moment do they begin to play the mysterious?

The instant philosophy, more precisely the name philosophy, lost its first signification, "*seine erste Bedeutung.*" And this primitive signification—Kant does not doubt this for a single instant—is "scientific wisdom of life," literally a wisdom of life regulating itself according to a knowledge or a science (*wissenschaftlichen Lebensweisheit*) [8:389]. The mystagogues get hold of the name philosophy the instant it loses its signification or its original reference, that name from then on empty or usurped, that pseudonym or that cryptonym, which is first a homonym. And that does not fail to occur in a regular, recurrent way, ever since the sense was lost: this is not the first time. To be sure, Kant is more closely interested in some recent examples of this mystagogic and psychagogic imposture, but he supposes at the outset that the usurpation is recurrent and obeys a law. There has been and will always be philosophical mystification, speculation on the end and the ends of philosophy. This depends on an event that Kant himself does not date and that he seems to situate right up against the origin, namely, that the name philosophy can circulate without its original *reference,* in other words without its *Bedeutung* and without guarantee of its value. While still remaining in the Kantian axiomatic, as it were, we can already infer from this that no harm would have happened [*arrivé*], no mystagogic speculation would have been credible or efficient, nothing or no one would have detoned [*détonné*] in philosophy without this errance of the name far from the thing, and if the relation of the name philosophy to its originary sense had been insured against every accident.

So some slackness was indeed necessary in this relation of sign to thing in order to contrive the space for a rerouting of sense or the grip for a perversion. Too slack a reference, then, there where it should be tighter, more exact, more rigorous. Here I hand you an association that will perhaps seem verbal, but since the lack of rigor or tension in the verbalization is already our concern, it occurs to me that *tonos,* tone, first signified the tight ligament, cord, rope when it is woven or braided, cable, strap—briefly, the privileged figure of everything subject to strict-ure. *Tonion* is the ligament as band and surgical bandage. In short, the same tension runs across tonic difference (that which under the word *strict-ure* forms both the theme and the instrument, the cord of *Glas*[3] and tonal difference, the deviation, the changes or mutation of tones (Hölderlin's *Wechsel der Töne* constituting one of the most obsessive motifs of *The Post Card*[4]). From this value of tension, or of elasticity (for example in a ballistic machine), we pass to the idea of tonic accent, of rhythm, of mode (Dorian, Phrygian, etc.). The tone's pitch is tied to tension; it has a bond to the bond, to the bond's more or less tight tension. This is not sufficient for determining the sense of the word *tone* when it is a matter of the voice. Even less when, through a great number of figures and tropical displacements, the tone of a discourse or of a piece in writing is analyzed in terms of content, manners of speaking, connotations, rhetorical staging, and pose taken, in semantic, pragmatic, scenographic terms, and so on; in short, rarely or not at all, in tuning in to the pitch of a voice or to a quality of timbre. I close this parenthesis.

So the bond fastening the name philosophy to its signification really had to be slackened for the philosophical title to be regularly available as a simple ornament, adornment, decoration, costume, or ceremonial dress (*Ausschmückung*), a signifier usurped and treated as intellectual travesty, as intellectual transvestism by those Kant nonetheless calls thinkers, and thinkers self-styled uncommon.

These people place themselves out of the common, but they have this in common: they say they are in immediate and intuitive relation with a mystery. And they wish to attract, seduce, lead toward the mystery and by the mystery. *Mysta-*

gogein is indeed this: to lead, initiate into the mystery; that is the mystagogue's or the initiatory priest's function. This *agogic* function of the leader of men, of *duce,* of *Führer,* of *leader* places him above the crowd he manipulates through the intermediary of a small number of followers gathered into a sect with a crypted language, a band, a clique or a small party with its ritualized practices. The mystagogues claim to possess as if in private the privilege of a mysterious *secret* (*Geheimnis* is the word that recurs most often). The revelation or unveiling of the secret is reserved to them; they jealously protect it. Jealousy is a major trait here. They never transmit the secret to others in everyday language, only by initiation or inspiration. The mystagogue is *philosophus per initiationem* or *per inspirationem.* Kant envisages a whole differential list and a historical typology of these mystagogues, but he recognizes in all of them one common trait: they never fail to take themselves for lords (*sich für* Vornehme *halten*), elite beings, distinguished subjects, superior and apart in society. Whence a series of value oppositions I am content to indicate very quickly: they scoff at [*prennent de haut*] work, the concept, schooling; to what is given they believe they have access effortlessly, gracefully, intuitively or through genius, outside of school. They are partisans of intellectual intuition, and the whole Kantian systematic could be recognized, though I shall not do so here, in his lampoon [*libelle*]. The hierarchized opposition of gift to work, of intuition to concept, of genius's mode to scholar's mode (*geniemäßig/schulmäßig*) [8:390] is homologous to the opposition between aristocracy and democracy, eventually between demagogic oligarchy and authentic rational democracy. Masters and slaves: the overlord reaches with a leap and through feeling what is immediately given him; the people work, elaborate, conceive.

And there we approach the more acute problem of tone. Kant does not find fault with true aristocrats, with persons truly *vornehme,* with authentic distinction, only with those who give or take themselves for distinguished beings, with the grant air of those pretentious people who elevate their voice, with those who raise the tone in philosophy. Kant does not incriminate the lofty pitch of the overlordly tone when it is just, natural, or legitimate. He takes aim at the rise in tone when an upstart [*parvenu*] authorizes himself to do so by giving himself airs and by sporting usurped signs of social membership. So the satire aims at the mimicry and not the tone itself. For a tone can be mimicked, feigned, faked. I shall go so far as to say *synthesized.*

But what does the fiction of the tone presuppose? How far can that fiction go? Here I am going to force and accelerate a bit of interpretation beyond commentary. A tone can be taken, and taken from the other. To change voice or mimick the intonation of the other, one must be able to confuse or induce a confusion between two voices, two voices of the other and, necessarily, of the other in oneself. How is one to discriminate the voices of the other in oneself? Instead of engaging myself directly in this immense problem, I return to the Kantian text and to a figure that seems to belong to the current rhetoric and to so-called used up [*usées*] metaphors. The question concerns the distinction between the voice of reason and the voice of the oracle. (Perhaps here I shall echo, without being sure I am responding to, the questioning, the injunction, or the request Jean-Luc Nancy addressed to me the other day.)

Kant is lenient with highly placed persons who devote themselves to philosophy, even if they do so badly, who multiply the faults against the School and believe they reach the peaks of metaphysics. They have a certain merit; they have condescended to mingle with the others and to philosophize "in the same shoes of civic equality" (bourgeois, *bürgerlichen* equality) [8:394]. On the other hand, philosophers by profession are unpardonable when they play the overlord and take on grand airs. Their crime is properly political; it is a matter for [*relève de*] a kind of police. Further on, Kant will speak of "the police in the realm of the sciences (*die Polizei im Reiche der Wissenschaften*)" [8:404]. The police will have to stay vigilant to suppress—symbolically—not only the individuals who improperly adorn themselves with the title of philosopher, who take hold of and bedeck themselves [*s'emparent et se parent*] with the overlordly tone in philosophy, but also those who flock around them; for that haughtiness [*morgue*] with which one settles on the peaks of metaphysics, that wordy arrogance is contagious; it gives rise to aggregations, congregations, and chapels. This dream of a knowledge police could be related to the plan for a university tribunal presented in *The Conflict of Faculties*.[5] The tribunal was intended to arbitrate the conflicts between the provisionally lower faculty (the faculty of philosophy) and the higher faculties, so called because they represent the power whose official instrument they are (theology, law, and medicine). This tribunal is also a parliament of knowledge. And philosophy, which has the right to inspect everything touching on the truth of theoretical (constative) propositions but no power to give orders, occupies in the parliament the bench on the left and in the conflicts concerning practical reason has the authority only to treat formal questions. The other questions, the most serious for existence, are a matter for the higher faculties, singularly theology. In the indictment before us, philosophers by profession are not pardoned when they take on a tone, overlordly because, in raising thus the tone, they hoist themselves above their colleagues or comrades (*Zunftgenossen*) [8:394], and wrong them in their inalienable right to freedom and equality regarding everything touching on reason alone. And they do this precisely—here's what I was wanting to come to—by perverting the voice of reason, by mixing the two voices of the other in us, the voice of reason and the voice of the oracle. Those people believe work to be useless in philosophy: it would suffice to "listen to . . . the oracle within oneself (*nur das Or-*

akel in sich selbst anhören)" [8:390]. These are Kant's first words.

Since this voice speaks to them in private, through what is properly their idiomatic feeling, their desire or their pleasure, they make it say what they want. On the other hand, you do not make the voice of reason say just anything. These are the lampoon's last words: the voice of an oracle (*die Stimme eines Orakels*) always lends itself to all kinds of interpretations (*Auslegungen*) [8:405]. The priest-mystagogues are also interpreters; the element of their agogic power is the hermeneutic or hermetic seduction (and here one thinks of what Warburton said about the political power in ancient Egypt of the scribes and of the priests as decipherers of hieroglyphs).[6] The overlordly tone dominates and is dominated by the oracular voice that covers over the voice of reason, rather parasitizes it, causes it to derail or become delirious. To raise the tone, in this case, is to make it jump, is to make the inner voice delirious, the inner voice that is the voice of the other in us. The word *delirium* appears once in Latin, in citing the verse of a monk of the Middle Ages (*Quaerit delirus, quod non respondet Homerus* [8:393]), and one other time in the French translation (here I find it a little forced but interesting) for a word that interests me even more, *Verstimmung.*

Guillermit translates *Verstimmung der Köpfe zur Schwärmerei* [8:398] as *délire de têtes qui s'exaltent* [*D'un ton,* 99] 'delirium in the heads of those who exalt themselves,' and he is right. The overlordly tone is authorized by a *salto mortale* (which is also Kant's expression [8:398]), a leap from concepts to the unthinkable or the irrepresentable, an obscure anticipation of the mysterious secret come from beyond. This leap toward the imminence of a vision without concept, this impatience turned toward the most crypted secret sets free a poetico-metaphorical overabundance. To that extent this overabundance has indeed an apocalyptic affinity, but Kant never speaks the word for reasons we shall glimpse in a moment. *Verstimmen,* which Guillermit translates not without reason by *délirer* 'to be delirious,' is first of all to put out of tune [*désaccorder*], when speaking of a stringed instrument [*instrument à cordes*] and, or again, for example, a voice. This is currently said of a piano. Less strictly this signifies derange, put out of order, jumble. One is delirious when one is deranged in the head. *Verstimmung* can come to spoil a *Stimmung:* pathos, or the humor that then becomes testy. The *Verstimmung* we are speaking about here is indeed a social disorder and a derangement, an out-of-tune-ness [*désaccordement*] of strings and voices in the head. The tone leaps and rises when the voice of the oracle, uncovering your ear, jumbling, covering, or parasitizing the voice of reason equally speaking in each and using the same language with everyone, takes you aside, speaks to you in a private code, and whispers secrets to you. The voice of reason, Kant says, *die Stimme der Vernunft,* speaks to each without equivocation (*deutlich*) and gives access to scientific knowledge. But it is essentially for giving orders and prescribing. For if we had the time to reconstitute the whole internal and properly Kantian necessity of this address, we would have to go as far as the extreme finesse of the objection made to the mystagogues. Not only do they confuse the voice of the oracle with that of reason. They do not distinguish either between pure speculative reason and pure practical reason; they believe they *know* what is solely *thinkable* and reach through feeling alone the universal laws of practical reason. So there is a voice of practical reason; it describes nothing; it says nothing describable; it dictates, prescribes, orders. Kant also names it in Latin: *dictamen rationis* [8:402]. Although it gives rise to autonomy, the law it dictates is as little flexible, as little subject to free interpretation as if it came from the completely other in me. It is a "brazen voice" [8:402, translation modified], Kant says. It resounds in every man, for every man has in him the idea of duty. And it resounds rather loudly in him; it strikes rather percussively and repercussively; it even thunders in him, for man trembles (*zittert*) to hear this brazen voice that, from the height of its majesty, orders him to sacrifice his drives, to resist seductions, to forgo his desires. And the voice promises me nothing in return; it assures me no compensation. It is sublime in this; it orders, mandates, demands, commands without giving anything in exchange; it thunders in me to the point of making me tremble; it thus provokes the greatest questions and the greatest astonishment (*Erstaunen*) [8:402]. That is the *true* mystery. Kant also calls it *Geheimnis* [8:403], but it is no longer the mystery of the mystagogues. It is the mystery at once domestic, intimate, and transcendent, the *Geheimnis* of practical reason, the sublimity of moral law and moral voice. The mystagogues fail to recognize that *Geheimnis;* they confuse it with a mystery of vision and contact, whereas the moral law never gives itself to be seen or touched. In this sense, the *Geheimnis* of moral law is more in tune with the essence of the voice that hears/understands itself but neither touches nor sees itself, thus seeming to hide itself from every external intuition. But in its very transcendence the moral voice is nearer, and thus more autoaffective, more autonomous. The moral law then is more auditory, more audible than the mystagogic oracle still contaminated by feeling, illumination, or intuitive vision, contact and mystical tact ("*ein . . . mystischer Takt,*" Kant says [8:398]). The overlordly tone detones because it is foreign to the essence of the voice.

Why did I feel inclined, at this moment of my reading of an overlordly tone, to add this piece to the dossier (if I can say that) of *The Post Card?* Or again to file it in what is called *dossier* therein, between the word and the thing, the word *dossier* packed with all the *dos* [back, *do,* etc.] whose note and syllable punctuate the "Envois" on each page, at Socrates' back and on the back of the postcard, with all the words in *do* and with the back [*dossier*] of the chair, of the partition between Plato and Socrates when the latter seems to write what the former dictates? Not only on account of the mixing or changing of tones (*Wechsel der Töne*) that would form in this book at once a theme and a manner. Nor on account of the word and the thing "apocalypse" that regularly recur there, with the numerological obsession and the insistence of the number 7 that also gives rhythm to John's Apocalypse. The signer of the "Envois" mocks what he calls "my post card apocalypse," our "small, library apocalypse" (*The Post Card,* 13, 11). Nor is this the satire of academic philosophy. No, at this point of my reading of "an overlordly tone," what I did feel inclined to add to *The Post Card*'s dossier is the difficulty Plato gives to Kant, the devilish job Kant gives himself with Plato, the untiring rhetoric for distinguishing between the good Plato and the bad Plato, the true and the false, his authentic writings and his more or less reliable or apocryphal ones.

That is to say, his Letters. Kant wants at once to accuse and excuse Plato of this continuous catastrophe that has corrupted philosophy, the strict relation between the name and the thing "philosophy," which ends up in this detoning *Verstimmung.* He wants to accuse *and* excuse him of delirium in philosophy, one would say in the same movement of a double postulation. *Double bind* again of filiation: Plato is the father of the delirium, of all exaltation in philosophy ("*der Vater aller Schwärmerei* mit der Philosophie"), but without it having been his fault ("*ohne seine Schuld*"). So we must divide Plato; we must distinguish between the Academic and the presumed author of the Letters, the teacher and the sender [*envoyeur*].

> Plato the *academic* was, therefore, although it was not his fault (for he used his intellectual intuitions only backward, to *explain* the possibility of synthetic knowledge a priori, not forward, to *widen* this knowledge through such intuition into Ideas readable [*lesbare*] in the divine intellect [the innocent Plato is Kant's

> father, as well as the postcard[2] of a self-portrait by Kant; the innocent Plato is not the father of delirium]), the father of all exaltation in *philosophy.* But I would not at all want to confuse Plato the *letter writer* (*Plato den* Briefsteller) (newly translated into German) with Plato the academic. [8:398]

Kant's pamphlet, which came out in the *Berlinische Monatsschrift,* is dead set against a certain Schlosser who had just translated the Letters of Plato, in a work entitled *Plato's Letters on the Revolution in Syracuse, with a Historical Introduction and Notes* (1795). Kant seems to denounce Schlosser *directly* when he appeals to Plato and certain of his so-called esoteric doctrines; but *indirectly,* we know he wants to get at Jacobi. And what is intolerable in this letter writer Plato is aristocratic esotericism—Kant cites that Letter recommending that secrets not be divulged to the crowd—a cryptophilia combined with a mystical interpretation of mathematics. The great stake between Plato and Kant is, of course, the philosophical interpretation of mathematics. Plato, enchanted by geometric figures, as Pythagoras was by numbers [*nombres*], would have done nothing but have a presentiment of the problematic of the a priori synthesis and too quickly would have taken refuge in a mysticism of geometry, as Pythagoras in the mysticism of numbers. And this mathematizing mysticism, this idolatry of figures and numbers [*chiffres*] always goes hand in hand with the phenomena of sect, cryptopolitics, indeed superstitious theophany that Kant opposes to rational theology. Numerology, mystic illumination, theophanic vision—all that indeed belongs to the apocalyptic world. And here I note in passing that, in the vast and overabundant corpus of the apocalyptic "genre," from the Persian and Zoroastrian heritage up to the very numerous Jewish and Christian apocalypses, the experts often inscribe

[2] I am thinking of that bust of Kant "in the Greek style" (Emanuel Bardou, 1798) reproduced on a postcard in a Berlin museum.

this or that text of Plato, especially the myth of Er in the *Republic*. This apocalyptic corpus has been collected, identified, and studied as such only in the nineteenth century. Kant never names the Apocalypse in this text, but he does make, three years earlier, a brief allusion to it, between parentheses, in *Religion within the Limits of Reason Alone*—which is one of the most indispensable contextual surroundings for understanding the essay "On a Newly Arisen Superior Tone in Philosophy." In this parenthesis, the Apocalypse is invoked in order to designate the punishment of the guilty ones at the end of the world as the end of history (book 3, division 2, "Historical Account of the Gradual Establishment of the Sovereignty of the Good Principle on Earth";[7] also cf. *Conflict of Faculties*, 113).

This cryptopolitics is also a cryptopoetics, a poetic perversion of philosophy.

And it is again a matter of the veil and of castration.

Eight years ago, right here in fact, I had spoken of veil and castration, of interpreters, of hermeneutics and hermetics. "I have forgotten my umbrella" is a statement at once hermetic and totally open, as secret and superficial as the postcard apocalypse it announces and protects against.[8] And elsewhere, in *Glas* [187, 256] and in "Economimesis,"[9] I had indicated the intrigue of a certain veil of Isis around which Kant and Hegel had more than once busied themselves. I am going to expose myself to taking (and tying) up again with the threads of this intrigue and with the treatment of castration, faced with Isis.

On the veil of Isis and on castration Kant says nothing that visibly refers them to each other within the same demonstrative argument. I observe only a kind of tropical continuity, but the tropical transfer(ence), the metaphorical and the analogical, is exactly our problem.

The mystagogues of modernity, according to Kant, do not simply tell us what they see, touch, or feel. The *have a pre-*

sentiment of, they anticipate, they approach, they smell out, they are the men of imminence and the trace. For example, they say they have a presentiment of the sun and cite Plato. They say that every philosophy of men can point to or designate the dawn, but that one can have only a presentiment of the sun. Kant is ironical about this presentiment of the sun; he multiplies his sarcastic remarks. These new Platonists give us through sentiment or presentiment (*Gefühl, Ahnung*) only a theatrical sun (*Theatersonne*), a chandelier in sum [*un lustre en somme*]. And then these people abuse metaphors, figurative expressions (*bildliche Ausdrücke*) [8:399], in order to sensitize us, to make us presensitive to this presentiment.

Here is an example of this—Kant cites his adversaries: "to approach so near the goddess wisdom that one can perceive the *rustle* of her garment" [8:399] (its rustling [*Rauschen*], rather than its light touch [*frôlement*] as the French translation says [*D'un ton,* 101]). Or again: "since he cannot lift up the veil of Isis, he can nevertheless make it so thin (*so dünne*) that one can *have a presentiment of* the goddess under this veil (*unter ihm*)" [8:399, translation modified]. To lift up the veil of Isis here is *aufheben* (*da er den Schleier der Isis nicht aufheben kann*), and one can still dream between the *gala* of this *Aufhebung* and that apocalyptic unveiling.

Kant fires off his dart [*son trait*]: thin to what point, he asks; that we are not told. Probably not thin enough, still too thick, so that one can do what one wants with the ghost (*Gespenst*) behind its veil or sheet. For otherwise, if the veil were absolutely thin, and transparent, this would be a vision, a seeing (*Sehen*), and, Kant notes in quite mercilessly taking aim, that must be avoided (*vermieden*). Above all, we must not see; we must have only a presentiment under the veil. Then our mystagogues play on the ghost and the veil; they replace the evidences and proofs with "analogies," "probabilities" (*Analogieen, Wahrscheinlichkeiten*) [8:399]. These are their words. Kant cites them and calls us to witness: you see, they are not true philosophers; they resort to poetic schemas. All that [*ça*] is so much literature. We know this scene well today, and it is, among other things, to this repetition that I would like to draw your attention. Not to take sides or come to a decision—I shall do no such thing—between metaphor and concept, literary mystagogy and true philosophy, but for a start to recognize the old solidarity of these antagonists or protagonists.

Consider now that Kant first proposes the word or the image of castration, or more rigorously of "emasculating (*Entmannung*)" [8:399], as one example of those "analogies" or "probabilities" that this "new mystical-Platonic language" [8:398] abuses to manipulative ends. He first takes them from a sentence of that Schlosser who just translated and introduced Plato's Letters. Nietzsche might have made something of this name Schlosser, as he did of Schleiermacher, the first "maker of" hermeneutic "veils." Schlosser is the locksmith, the man who makes or keeps the keys, true or false, but also the official in charge of locking up, the one who closes and knows all about closure, expert as he is in speaking of it, in producing it, or in getting the better of it. This Schlosser, then, had spoken, by figure, of "emasculating . . . reason (*Entmannung der . . . Vernunft*)," and he had accused "metaphysical sublimation (*metaphysische Sublimation*)" of this emasculation. An inadmissible analogy in Kant's eyes, abusive because it takes the place of proof by coming to the place where the demonstration leaves a "lack (*Mangel*)," but also scandalous because in truth those who adorn themselves with this new tone in philosophy are they who emasculate and make a corpse of reason. "For the purpose of argumentation," he says, "since there is a lack of rigorous proofs, the following are offered as arguments: 'analogies, probabilities' (which were discussed above), thus 'the danger of emasculating [the French translation [*D'un ton*, 101] says "castration" for "emasculating"] a faculty of reason that has become so high-strung by metaphysical sublimation that it can hardly maintain itself in the struggle with vice.' " And Kant immediately turns the argument inside out, I would say like a glove: "Whereas," he says, "it is in precisely these a priori principles that practical reason rightly feels its otherwise never intimated strength, and it is, on the other hand, in falsely attributed empirical properties (which are, for precisely this reason, unfit for universal legislation) that reason is emasculated and paralyzed (*entmannt und gelähmt*)" [8:399–400, translation modified] ("castrated and paralyzed" in *D'un ton,* 104).

If castration is a metaphor or a simulacrum—and so it must be, it seems, since it concerns the phallus, not the penis or the clitoris—then the metaphorical stake is clear between the two opposing parties sketched out [*campés*] by a Kant who is no less a party in this. The stake for this *Kampfplatz* of metaphysics is the castration of reason. Which of the two parties facing each other most surely castrates reason? Or more seriously: which of the two unmans, *entmannt,* this descendant of *logos* that is *ratio?* Each of the two—we just heard them without the least equivocation—would accuse the other of castrating the *logos* and of defalcating its phallus. And into this debate, phallogocentric on both sides, therefore throughout, we could put Freud on the scene as a third robber procuring the key (true or false), "sexual theory," namely, that for this stage of reason in which there is only male reason, only a masculine *or* castrated organ or canon of reason, everything proceeds in this just as for that stage of infantile genital organization in which there is definitely a masculine but no feminine. Perhaps he would speak of a *phallic stage* of reason. "The antithesis here," Freud says at the end of "The Infantile Genital Organization," "is between having a male genital and being castrated."[10] No sexual difference [*pas de différence*] as opposition, but only the masculine! This strange logic (reason since Freud, Lacan would say) could be followed quite far into the details of the text, above all in the moments when the veil of Isis unleashes what Freud calls *Bemächtigungstrieb,* the drive for mastery. Kant, for example, accuses the mystagogic metaphysicians of behaving like "strong men (*Kraftmännern*)" who lately preach with enthusiasm a wisdom that costs them nothing, since they claim they have caught this goddess by the end of her robe and thus have made themselves her masters and lords; they would have "mastered (*bemächtigt*)" her [8:401n, translation modified], and so on.

The castration or not of *logos* as *ratio* is a central form of this debate around metaphysics. It is also a fight around the poetic (between poetry and philosophy), around the death or the future of philosophy. The stake is the same. Kant does not doubt this: the new preachers need to pervert philosophy into poetry in order to give themselves grand airs, to occupy through simulacrum and mimicry the place of the great, to usurp thus an essentially symbolic power.

Schlosser, the locksmith, we could say, right here, the man of the lordly castle, not only abuses poetic metaphors. He accuses his century of being prosaic, and he dares to write to Plato, addresses him, invokes him, apostrophizes him, calls him to witness: "*Armer Plato,* poor Plato, if you did not have the seal of Antiquity about you . . . who would still want to read you in this *prosaic* age in which the highest wisdom is to see nothing but what lies at our feet and to assume nothing but what we can grasp with our hands?" Locked in combat with Schlosser, who thrashes the new sons of the earth, Kant plays Aristotle against Plato: "But this conclusion unfortunately does not follow; it proves too much. For *Aristotle,* an extremely prosaic philosopher, certainly has the seal (*Siegel*) of antiquity about him, and according to the principle stated above, he has a claim to being read!—At bottom, all philosophy is indeed prosaic; and the suggestion that we should now start to philosophize poetically (*wiederum poetisch zu philosophieren*) would be just as welcome as the suggestion that a businessman (*Kaufmann*) should in the future no longer write his account books in prose but in verse" [8:406n].

But the strategy on both sides is more twisted still. The mystagogues, the analogists, and the anagogists—they too play the Aristotle card. And at that moment of play it is a matter of the ends and the end of philosophy. The wake [*la veillée*] over the death or the end of philosophy, the vigil [*la veille*] by the corpse of philosophy is not just an ancient (hi)story because it would date back to Kant. For it was already said that if philosophy were finished, that was not a deferred action [*un aprés-coup*] of the Kantian limitation or of the bounds [*termes*] placed on the empire of metaphysics, but already "two thousand years ago." Already two thousand years ago we finished with philosophy, said a disciple of Schlosser, a real count, this one, Count Leopold Stolberg, because "the Stagirite has conquered so much for science that he has left behind little of importance for his followers to espy" [8:394n].

Kant's rejoinder is that of a decided progressive; he believes in philosophy's finally open and unveiled future. It is also the response of an egalitarian democrat: you want to put an end to philosophy through obscurantism (*durch Obscuriren*) [8:394n], and you are disguised monarchists; you want all to be equal among themselves, but with the exception of one single individual, all are nothing. Sometimes the individual is Plato, sometimes Aristotle, but in truth through this monarchism you play the philosophers and elevate yourselves by proclaiming the end of philosophy in an overlordly tone.

Naturally, even when he fights like this, Kant declares that he does not like war. As in *The Conflict of Faculties* (in which he distinguished moreover between natural warfare and the conflict arbitrated by a law), he ends by proposing to the castrating adversary a kind of concordat, a deal, a peace treaty, or a contract—in short, the solution of a conflict that is not an antinomy. As you have perhaps foreseen, this contract is more important to me than the whole combinatory strategy, the play, and the exchange of places. What can deeply bind the two opposing parties and procure for them a neutral ground of reconciliation for speaking together again in a fitting tone? In other words, what do they together exclude as the inadmissible itself? What is the *inadmissible?*

Kant speaks of modernity, and of the mystagogues of his time, but you will have quickly perceived in passing, without my even having to designate explicitly, name, or draw out all the threads, how many transpositions we could indulge in on the side of *our* so-called modernity. I will not say that today everyone would recognize him- or herself on this or that side, purely and simply. But I am sure it could be demonstrated that today every slightly organized discourse is found or claims to be found on both sides, alternately or simultaneously, even if this emplacement exhausts nothing, does not go round the turn or the contour [*ne fait pas le tour ou le contour*] of the place and the discourse held. And this inadequation, always limited itself, no doubt indicates the densest difficulty. Each of us is the mystagogue *and* the *Aufklärer* of an other. I leave it to you to try some of these transpositions; we could return to them in the discussion.

What, then, is the contract? What condition does Kant lay down for those who, like himself, declare their concern to speak the truth, to *reveal* without emasculating the *logos?* For they agree on this together, this is the place of consensus where they can meet and come together, their synagogue. Kant first asks them to get rid of the veiled goddess before which they both tend to kneel. He asks them no longer to personify the moral law or the voice that incarnates it. No longer, he says to the mystagogues, should we personify the law that speaks in us, above all not in the "esthetic," sensible, and beautiful form of this veiled Isis. Such will be the condition for understanding/hearing the moral law itself, the unconditioned, and for understanding/hearing ourselves and getting along [*pour nous entendre*]. In other words—and this is a trenchant motif for thought of the law or of the ethical today—Kant calls for placing the law above and beyond, not the person, but personification and the body, above and beyond, as it were, the sensible voice that speaks in us, the singular voice that speaks to us in private, the voice that could be said in his language to be "pathological" in opposition to the voice of reason. The law above the body, above this body found here to be represented by a veiled goddess. Even if you do not want to grant some *signifiance* or "significance" to the fact that what the concordat excludes is precisely the body of a veiled Isis, the universal principle of feminity, murderess of Osiris, all of whose pieces she later recovers, except for the phallus. Even if you also think that that is a personification too analogical or metaphorical, grant me at least this: the truce proposed between the two declared defenders of a nonemasculated *logos* supposes some exclusion. It supposes some *inadmissible*. There is an excluded middle and that will be enough for me.

Enough for me in view of what? Before pursuing this question, I shall read the proposition of peace or alliance addressed by Kant to his adversaries of the day, but perhaps to his accomplices of all times:

> But what is the good of all this conflict between two parties that at bottom share one and the same intention: to make people wise and virtuous? It is much noise about nothing, disunity out of a misunderstanding in which no reconciliation but only a reciprocal clarification is needed in order to conclude a treaty that makes future concord even more heartfelt.
>
> The veiled goddess for whom we of both parties bend our knees is the moral law in us, in its inviolable majesty. We do indeed perceive her voice and also understand very well her command. But when we are listening, we are in doubt whether

> it comes from man, from the perfected power of his own reason, or whether it comes from an other, whose nature is unknown to us and speaks to man through this, his own reason. At bottom we would perhaps do better to rise above and thus spare ourselves research into this matter; since such research is only speculative and since what obliges us (objectively) to act remains always the same, one may place one or the other principle down as a foundation. But the didactic procedure of bringing the moral law within us into clear concepts according to a logical methodology is the only authentically *philosophical* one, whereas the procedure whereby the law is personified and reason's moral bidding is made into a veiled Isis (even if we attribute to her no other properties than those that were discovered according to the method above), is an *aesthetic* mode of representing (*eine* ästhetische *Vorstellungsart*) precisely the same object; one can doubtless use this mode of representation backward, after the first procedure has already purified the principles, in order to enliven those ideas by a sensible, albeit only analogical, presentation (*Darstellung*), and yet one always runs the danger of falling into an exalting vision [*schwärmerische Vision*], which is the death of all philosophy. [8:405]

Among the numerous traits characterizing an apocalyptic type of writing [*écrit*], let us provisionally isolate prediction and eschatological preaching [*prédication*], the fact of telling, foretelling, or preaching the end, the extreme limit, the imminence of the last. Can one not say then that all the parties to such a concordat are the subjects of eschatological discourses? No doubt, other contexts taken into account, this situation is older than the Copernican revolution; the numerous prototypes of apocalyptic discourses would suffice to attest to this, as would so many others in the meantime. But if Kant denounces those who proclaim that philosophy has been at an end for two thousand years, he has himself, in marking a limit, indeed the end of a certain type of metaphysics, freed another wave of eschatological discourses in philosophy. His progressivism, his belief in the future of a certain philosophy, indeed of another metaphysics, is not contradictory to this proclamation of ends and of the end.

And I shall now start again from this fact: from then on and with multiple and profound differences, indeed mutations, being taken into account, the West has been dominated by a powerful program that was also an untransgressible contract among discourses of the end. The themes of the end of history and the death of philosophy represent [*figurent*] only the most comprehensive, massive, and gathered forms of this. To be sure, there are obvious differences between Hegelian eschatology, that Marxist eschatology that people have too quickly wanted to forget these last years in France (and perhaps this was another eschatology *of Marxism,* its eschatology and its death knell [*glas*]), Nietzschean eschatology (between the last man, the higher man, and the overman), and so many other, more recent varieties. But aren't these differences measured as deviations in relation to the fundamental tonality of this *Stimmung* audible across so many thematic variations? Haven't all the differences [*différends*] taken the form of a going-one-better in eschatological eloquence, each newcomer more lucid than the other, more vigilant and more prodigal too, coming to add more to it: I tell you this in truth; this is not only the end of this here but also and first of that there, the end of history, the end of the class struggle, the end of philosophy, the death of God, the end of religions, the end of Christianity and morals (that [*ça*], that was the most serious naïveté), the end of the subject, the end of man, the end of the West, the end of Oedipus, the end of the earth, *Apocalypse Now,* I tell you, in the cataclysm, the fire, the blood, the fundamental earthquake, the napalm descending from the sky by helicopters, like prostitutes, and also the end of literature, the end of painting, art as a thing of the past, the end of psychoanalysis, the end of the university, the end of phallocentrism and phallogocentrism, and I don't know what else? And whoever would come to refine, to say the finally final [*le fin du fin*], namely the end of the end [*la fin de la fin*], the end of ends, that the end has always already begun, that we must still distinguish between closure and end, that person would, whether wanting to or not, participate in the concert. For it is also the end of metalanguage on the subject of eschatological language. With the result that we can wonder if eschatology is a tone, or even the voice itself.

Isn't the voice always that of the last man? Voice or language [*langue*] itself, song or accent in language itself? Hölderlin closes his second version of *Patmos,* the poem bearing as its title the name of the apocalyptic island, that of John, by invoking the poem of the German tongue ("*Dem folgt deutscher Gesang*" ["This end German song purses"]). Heidegger often cites the first lines of this poem:

> Nah ist
> Und schwer zu fassen der Gott.
> Wo aber Gefahr ist, wächst
> Das Rettende auch.
>
> (Near and
> Hard to grasp is the God.
> But where danger is,
> Deliverance also grows.)[11]

And if Heidegger thinks the *Überwindung* of metaphysics or of ontotheology as that of the eschatology inseparable from it, he does so in the name of another eschatology. Several times he says of thought, here distinct from philosophy, that it is essentially "eschatological." That is his word.

Isn't the voice of language, I was asking, always that of the last man? Forgoing reading with you Blanchot's *Last Man,*[12] I recall, since I spoke of the voice and of Oedipus, this fragment from the *Philosophenbuch.* Nietzsche, under the title "Oedipus" and in an absolute soliloquy, has the last philosopher, who is also the last man, speak with himself. He speaks *with* his voice; he converses with himself [*s'entretient*] and maintains [*entretient*] what life remains for him with the phantom of his voice; and he calls (on) himself, he is called Oedipus: " 'I call myself the last philosopher, because I am the last man. No one speaks with me but myself, and my voice comes to me like the voice of a dying man! Let me associate for but one hour more with you, dear voice, with you, the last trace of the memory of all human happiness. With you I escape loneliness through self-delusion and lie myself into multiplicity and love. For my heart resists the belief that love is dead. It cannot bear the shudder of the loneliest loneliness, and so it forces me to speak as if I were two. . . .' "

" 'As if I were two' ": for the moment he thus sends himself this message by acting *as if* he could still really address it to himself; this impossible destination signs the death of the last man, in and outside him. He knows him beyond the *as if:* " 'And yet, I still hear you, dear voice! *Something* else dies, something other than me, the last man in this universe. The last sigh, *your* sigh, dies with me. The drawn-out "alas! alas!" sighed for me, Oedipus, the last miserable man.' "[13]

Then if eschatology surprises us at the first word, at the first as at the last, always at the last but one, what are we to say? What are we to do? The response to this question is perhaps impossible, because it never lets itself be expected. For the question is that of the response, and of a call promising or responding before the question.

Clarity is necessary, Philippe Lacoue-Labarthe said yesterday. Yes. But there is light, and there are lights, daylight, and also the madness of the day [*la folie du jour*]. "The end is beginning," we read in *The Madness of the Day.*[14] Without even referring to apocalypses of the Zoroastrian type (there were more than one of them), we know that every apocalyptic eschatology is promised in the name of light, of the visionary and vision, and of a light of light, of a light brighter than all the lights it makes possible. John's apocalypse, which dominates the whole of the Western apocalyptic, is lit by the light of El, of Elohim:

> yes, the glory of Elohim illuminates it.
> . . . .
>
> the kings of the earth bring their glory into it.
>
> Its gates are never closed for the day:
> no, there is no night there.
> They bring the glory.
>
> (21:23–26)
>
> Night is no more,
> they do not need lamplight
> nor sunlight:
> Adônaï Elohim illuminates them, and they
> rule to the ages of ages.
>
> (22:5)

There is light, and there are lights, the lights of reason or of *logos,* that are not, for all that, some other thing. And it is in the name of an *Aufklärung* that Kant, for example, undertakes to demystify the overlordly tone. In the light of today we cannot not have become the heirs of these *Lumières.* We cannot and we must not—this is a law and a destiny—forgo the *Aufklärung,* in other words, what imposes itself as the enigmatic desire for vigilance, for the lucid vigil, for elucidation, for critique and truth, but for a truth that at the same time keeps within itself some apocalyptic desire, this time as desire for clarity and revelation, in order to demystify or, if you prefer, to deconstruct apocalyptic discourse itself and with it everything that speculates on vision, the imminence of the end, theophany, parousia, the last judgment. Then each time, we intractably ask ourselves where they want to come to, and to what ends, those who declare the end of this or that, of man or the subject, of consciousness, of history, of the West or of literature, and according to the latest news, of progress itself, the idea of which has never been in such bad health to the right and the left? What effects do these noble, gentile [*gentils*] prophets or eloquent visionaries want to produce? In view of what immediate or adjourned benefit? What do they do, what do we do in saying this? To seduce or subjugate whom, intimidate or make whom come [*jouir*]? These effects and these benefits can be related to an individual or collective, conscious or unconscious speculation. They can be analyzed in terms of libidinal or political mastery, with all the differantial relays and thus all the economic paradoxes that overdetermine the idea of power or mastery and sometimes drag them into the abyss. Lucid analysis of these interests or of these calculations should mobilize a very great number and a great diversity of interpretative apparatus available today. It must and can do this, for our epoch would be rather superarmed in this regard. And a deconstruction, if it does not stop there, nonetheless never goes without some secondary work on the system that joins this superarmament to itself, that articulates, as is said, psychoanalysis to Marxism or to some Nietzscheanism; to the resources of linguistics, rhetoric, or pragmatics; to the theory of *speech acts;* to Heideggerian thought on the history of metaphysics, the essence of science or of technology. Such a demystification must give in [*se plier*] to the finest diversity of apocalyptic ruses. The interest or the calculation of these ruses can be so dissimulated under the desire for light, well hidden (*eukalyptus,* as is said of the tree whose calycine limb remains closed after flowering), well hidden under the avowed desire for revelation. And one dissimulation can hide another. The most serious thing, for then it is endless, the most fascinating thing, depends on this: the subject of eschatological discourse can have an interest in forgoing its own interest, can forgo everything in order to place yet its death on your shoulders and make you inherit in advance its corpse, that is, its soul, the subject hoping thus to arrive at its ends through the end, to seduce you on the spot by promising you to guard your guard in his absence.

I am not sure that there is just *one* fundamental *scene, one* great paradigm according to which, except for some deviations, all the eschatological strategies would regulate themselves. It would still be a philosophical, onto-eschato-teleological interpretation to say: the apocalyptic strategy is fundamentally one, its diversity is only a diversity of procedures [*procédés*], masks, appearances, or simulacra.

With this caution in mind, let us yield for a short time to the temptation of a fiction and imagine this fundamental scene. Let us imagine that there is *one* apocalyptic tone, a unity of the apocalyptic tone, and that *the* apocalyptic tone is not the effect of a generalized derailment, of a *Verstimmung* multiplying the voices and making the tones shift [*sauter*], opening each word to the haunting memory [*hantise*] of the other in an unmasterable polytonality, with grafts, intrusions, interferences [*parasitages*]. Generalized *Verstimmung* is the possibility for the other tone, or the tone of another, to come at no matter what moment to interrupt a familiar music. (Just as, I suppose, this is readily produced in analysis, but also elsewhere, when suddenly a tone come from one knows not where renders speechless, if this can be said, the tone that tranquilly seemed to determine (*bestimmen*) the voice and thus insure the unity of destination, the self-identity of some addressee [*destinataire*] or sender [*destinateur*]. *Verstimmung,* if that is henceforth what we call the derailment, the sudden change [*saute*] of tone, as one would say *la saute d'humeur* 'the sudden change of mood,' is the disorder or the delirium of destination (*Bestimmung*), but also the possibility of all emission. The unity of tone, if there were any, would certainly be the assurance of destination, but also death, another apocalypse.) So let us imagine that there is *one* apocalyptic tone and *one* fundamental scene. Then whoever takes on the apocalyptic tone comes to tell you or itself something. But what? I say "whoever takes," "whosoever takes," in order not to say "he who" or "she who," "those men who" or "those women who," and I do indeed say "tone," which one must be able to distinguish from all articulated discursive content. What tone means (to say) is not perforce what the discourse says, and either can always contradict, deny, make drift, or derail the other.

Whoever takes on the apocalyptic tone comes to signify to, if not tell, you something. What? The truth, of course, and to signify to you that it reveals the truth to you; tone is revelatory of some unveiling in process. Unveiling or truth, apophantics of the imminence of the end, of whatever comes down, finally, to the end of the world. Not only truth as the revealed truth of a secret on the end or of the secret of the end. Truth itself is the end, the destination, and that truth unveils itself is the advent of the end. Truth is the end of the instance of the last judgment. The structure of truth here would be apocalyptic. And that is why there would not be any truth of the apocalypse that is not the truth of truth.

Then whoever takes on the apocalyptic tone will be asked: with a view to what and to what ends? In order to lead where, right now or soon?

The end is beginning, signifies the apocalyptic tone. But to what ends does the tone signify this? The apocalyptic tone naturally wants to attract, to get to come, to arrive at this, to seduce in order to lead to this, in other words, to the place where the first vibration of the tone is heard, which is called, as will be one's want, subject, person, sex, desire (I think rather of a pure differential vibration, without support, insupportable). The end is soon, it is imminent, signifies the tone. I see it, I know it, I tell you, now you know, come. We're all going to die, we're going to disappear, and this death sentence [*cet arrêt de mort*] cannot fail to judge us, we're going to die, you and I, the others too, the goyim, the gentiles, and all the others, all those who don't share this secret with us, but they don't know it. It's as if they're already dead. We're alone in the world; I'm the only one able to reveal to you the truth or the destination; I tell you it; I give it to you; come, let us be for a moment, we who don't yet know who we are, a moment before the end the sole survivors, the only ones to stay awake; it will be so much better. We'll be a sect, we'll form a species, a sex or gender, a race (*Geschlecht*) all by ourselves, we'll give ourselves a name. (That is just a bit the Babel scene, of which we can speak again, but there is also a Babel in John's Apocalypse that would lead us to think, not on the side of the confusion of tongues or tones, but of prostitution, if we suppose such distinctions can be made. Babel the great is the mother of whores: "'Come. I shall show you the judgment / of the great whore'" (17:1).) They sleep, we stay awake.

This discourse, or rather this tone I translate into discourse, this tone of the vigil at the moment of the end, which is also that of the funeral watch, of the *Wake,* it always cites or echoes [*répercute*] in a certain way John's Apocalypse or at least the fundamental scene that already programs the Johannine writing. Thus, for example:

> "'I know your works:
> you are renowned for living,
> but you are dead.
>
> Stay awake! [*Esto vigilans,* says the Latin translation.]
> Strengthen what remains, so near dying. . . .
> . . . .
>
> If you do not stay awake,
> I shall come like a thief:
> you will not know at what hour I shall come upon you.'"
> (3:1–3)

I shall come: the coming is always to come. The *Adôn* named as the aleph and the tav, the alpha and the omega, is the one who has been, who is, and who comes, not who shall be, but who comes, which is the present of a to-come [*à-venir*]. *I am coming* means: I am going to come, I am to-come in the imminence of an "I am going to come," "I am in the process of coming," "I am on the point of going to come." "Who comes" (*ho erkhomenos*) is translated here in Latin by *venturus est* [1:8].

Jesus is the one who says, "Stay awake!" But it would be necessary, perhaps beyond or before a narratology, to unfold a detailed analysis of the narrative voice in the Apocalypse. I use the expression *narrative voice* in order to distinguish it, as Blanchot does, from the narrating voice, that of the identifiable subject, of the narrator or determinable sender in a narrative, a *récit.* In addition, I believe that all the "come"s resounding in the *récits* or *non-récits* of Blanchot also resound, harmonize with a certain "Come" (*erkhou, veni*) of the Johannine Apocalypse. Jesus is the one who says, " ""Stay awake. . . . I shall come upon you."' " But John is the one speaking, citing Jesus, or rather writing, appearing to transcribe what he says in recounting that he cites Jesus the moment Jesus dictates to him to write—which he does presently and which we read—to the seven communities, to the seven churches of Asia. Jesus is cited as the one who dictates without himself writing and says, " 'write, *grapson.*' " But even before John writes, saying presently that he writes, he hears as a dictation the great voice of Jesus—

> I, Yohanân. . . .
> I am in the island called Patmos,
> because of the word of Elohim and the testimony of
> Yéshoua'.
> I am in the breath (*en pneumati, in spiritu*), on the day of the
> Adôn.
> I hear behind me a great voice,
> like that of a shofar. It says:

> "What you see, write it into a volume,
> send it to the seven communities."
>
> [1:9–11]

Write and send, dictates the voice come from behind, behind John's back, like a shofar, *grapson eis biblion kai pempson, scribe in libro: et mitte septem ecclesiis. I see* and *I hear,* in the present tense in Chouraqui's translation, are in the past in the Greek and the Latin, which does not simplify the premises of an analysis.[3] Now, even before this narrative scene citing a dictation or literally a present inspiration, there was a preamble without narrative, or in any case narrating, voice, a kind of title or name tag [*médaille*] come from one knows not where and binding the apocalyptic disclosure to the sending, the dispatch [*envoi*]. These lines are properly

[3]The stake here—this goes without saying—can be very grave, above all in an eschatological or apocalyptic text. Chouraqui has clearly assumed his responsibility as translator; here one can only leave it to him:

> The most constant liberty I have taken with the Greek text concerns the verb tenses. Already Joüon had noted this: "The attention given to the Aramaic substratum is particularly useful for avoiding too mechanical a translation of the Greek tenses."
>
> The Greek verb conceives time above all as a function of a past, a present, and a future; the Hebrew or the Aramaic, on the contrary, instead of specifying the time of an action, describes its state under two modes: the finished and the unfinished. As Pedersen has seen so well, the Hebrew verb is essentially *intemporal,* that is, *omnitemporal.*
>
> I have tried, between two notions of time irreducible to each other, to resort most often to the present, which in contemporary French usage is a very supple, very ample, very evocative tense, whether in its normal use or in the form of the historic present or the prophetic present. ("Une nouvelle traduction du Nouveau Testament," Preface to *Un Pacte neuf,* 13)

the apocalypse as sending of the apocalypse, the apocalypse that sends itself:

> Disclosure of Yéshoua' the messiah (*Apokalupsis Jēsou Khristou*):
> Elohim gives it to him
> to show to his servants
> what will happen soon.
>
> He signifies it by sending it through his messenger (*esēmanen aposteilas dia tou angelou autou, significavit mittens per angelum suum*)
> to his servant Yohanân.
>
> [1:1–2]

So John is the one who already receives mail [*courrier*] through the further intermediary of a bearer who is an angel, a pure messenger. And John transmits a message already transmitted, testifies to a testimony that will again be that of another testimony, that of Jesus; so many sendings, *envois*, so many voices, and this puts many people on the line.

> He signifies it by sending it through his messenger
> to his servant Yohanân.
>
> He reports the testimony of the word of Elohim
> and the testimony of Yéshoua' the messiah,
> all he has seen.
>
> Joys of the reader, of the hearer
> of the words of the inspiration
> of those who keep what is written:
>
> yes, the time approaches, *o gar kairos engus, tempus enim prope est.*
>
> [1:2–3]

If, in a very insufficient and scarcely even preliminary way, I draw your attention to the narrative sending [*envoi*], the interlacing of voices and *envois* in the dictated or addressed writing, I do so because, in the hypothesis or the program of an intractable demystification of the apocalyptic tone, in the style of the *Lumières* or of an *Aufklärung* of the twentieth century, and if one wanted to unmask the ruses, traps, trickeries, seductions, machines of war and pleasure—in short, all the interests of the apocalyptic tone today—it would be necessary to begin by respecting this differential multiplication [*démultiplication*] of voices and tones that perhaps divides them beyond a distinct and calculable plurality. One does not know (for it is no longer of the order of knowing) to whom the apocalyptic sending returns; it leaps [*saute*] from one place of emission to the other (and a place is always determined *starting from* the presumed emission); it goes from one destination, one name, and one tone to the other; it always refers [*renvoie*] to the name and to the tone of the other that is there but as having been there and before yet coming, no longer being or not yet there in the present of the *récit*.

And there is no certainty that man is the exchange [*le central*] of these telephone lines or the terminal of this endless computer. No longer is one very sure who loans its voice and its tone to the other in the Apocalypse; no longer is one very sure who addresses what to whom. But by a catastrophic reversal here more necessary than ever, one can just as well think this: as soon as one no longer knows who speaks or who writes, the text becomes apocalyptic. And if the *envois* always refer [*renvoient*] to other *envois* without decidable destination, the destination remaining to come, then isn't this completely angelic structure, that of the Johannine apocalypse, isn't it also the structure of every scene of writing in general? This is one of the suggestions I wanted to submit for your discussion: wouldn't the apocalyptic be a transcendental condition of all discourse, of all experience even, of every mark or every trace? And the genre of writings called "apocalyptic" in the strict sense, then, would be only an example, an *exemplary* revelation of this transcendental structure. In that case, if the apocalypse reveals, it is first of all the revelation of the apocalypse, the self-presentation of the apocalyptic structure of language, of writing, of the experience of presence, in other words, of the text or of the mark in general: *that is, of the divisible* envoi *for which there is no self-presentation nor assured destination.*

But let's leave this, there is an apocalyptic *pli* [fold, envelope, letter, habit, message] here. Not only a *pli* as *envoi,* a *pli* inducing a tonal change [*changement*] and an immediate tonal duplicity in every apocalyptic voice. Not only a fold in the signifier *apocalyptic* that designates at times the content of the *récit* or of what is announced, namely, the end-of-the-world catastrophes and cataclysms, the upheavals, the thunderbolts and earthquakes, the fire, the blood, the mountain of fire and the sea of blood, the afflictions, the smoke, the sulphur, the burning, the multiplicity of tongues and kings, the beast, the sorcerers, Satan, the great whore of the Apocalypse, and so on; and at other times, it designates the announcement itself and no longer what is announced, the discourse revealing the to-come or even the end of the world rather than what it says, the truth of the revelation rather than the revealed truth.

But I am thinking of another *pli* we are also in, in the light of today: everything that can now inspire a de-mystifying desire regarding the apocalyptic tone, namely, a desire for light, for lucid vigilance, for the elucidating vigil, for truth—all that is already found on the way, and I shall say in apocalyptic transfer(ence), it is already a citation or a recitation of John or of what already programmed John's *envois,* when, for example, he writes, for a messenger, under the dictate of the great voice come from behind his back and extended like a shofar, like a ram's horn:

> To the messenger of the community in Ephesus, write:
> "He says this,
> he who seizes the seven stars in his right hand,
> he who walks amid the seven gold lamps.
>
> 'I know your works, your toil,
> your endurance:
> you cannot endure the wicked.
>
> You have tested those who call themselves envoys and are not
> (*tous legontas eautous apostolous kai ouk eisin, qui se dicunt apostolos esse, et non sunt*),
> you find them liars.
> . . . .
>
> But I have this against you:
> your first love, you have left it.'"
>
> (2:1–2, 4)

And the *envois* multiply, then the seven messengers come, up to the seventh, after which

> The temple of Elohim opens to the sky.
> The coffer of his pact appears in his temple.
> There come lightning flashes, voices,
> thunders,
> an earthquake, great hail.
>
> A great sign (*sēmeion mega*) appears in the sky:
> a woman enveloped in sun,
> the moon under her feet,
> and on her head a crown of twelve stars.
>
> (11:19–12:1)

So we, *Aufklärer* of modern times, we continue to denounce the impostor apostles, the "so-called envoys" not sent [*envoyés*] by anyone, the liars and unfaithful ones, the turgidity and the pomposity of all those charged with a historic mission of whom nothing has been requested and who have been charged with nothing. Shall we thus continue in the best apocalyptic tradition to denounce false apocalypses?

Since the habit [*pli*] has already been acquired, I am not going to multiply the examples; the end approaches, but the apocalypse is long-lived. The question remains and comes back: what can be the limits of a demystification?

No doubt one can think—I do—that this demystification must be led as far as possible, and the task is not modest. It is interminable, because no one can exhaust the overdeterminations and the indeterminations of the apocalyptic strategems. And above all because the ethicopolitical motif or motivation of these strategems is never reducible to some simple. I recall thus that their rhetoric, for example is not only destined to mislead the people rather than the powerful in order to arrive at retrograde, backward-looking, conservative ends. Nothing is less conservative than the apocalyptic genre. And as it is an apocalyptic, apocryphal, masked, coded *genre,* it can use the detour to mislead another vigilance, that of censorship. We know that apocalyptic writings increased the moment State censorship was very strong in the Roman Empire, and precisely to catch the censorship unawares. Now this possibility can be extended to all censorships, and not only to the political, and in politics to the official. Even if we remained with political censorship and were alert enough to know that it is not practiced only starting from specialized State lairs [*officines*], but everywhere, like a thousand-eyed Argus, in a majority, in an opposition, in a virtual majority, with respect to everything that does not let itself be centered [*cadrer*] by the logic of the current political discourse and of the conceptual oppositions legitimated by the contract between the legitimate adversaries, well, then we would perhaps think that apocalyptic discourse can also get round censorship thanks to its genre and its cryptic ruses. By its very tone, the mixing of voices, genres, and codes, apocalyptic discourse can also, in dislocating [*détraquant*] destinations, dismantle the dominant contract or concordat. It is a challenge to the established receivability [*la recevabilité*] of messages and to the policing of destination, in short, to the postal police or the monopoly of posts. Conversely, we could even say that every discord or every tonal disorder, everything that detones and becomes inadmissible [*irrecevable*] in general collocution, everything that is no longer identifiable starting from established codes, from both sides and of a front, will necessarily pass for mystagogic, obscurantistic, and apocalyptic. It will be made to pass for such.

If we now inquire about another limit of demystification, a limit (perhaps) more essential that would (perhaps) distinguish a deconstruction from a simple progressive demystification in the style of the Enlightenment, I would be tempted by another bearing [*démarche*]. For finally, to demystify the seductive or agogic maneuver is fine and necessary, but must we not first ask ourselves with a view to what, to what end it [*ça*] seduces, uses trickery, misleads, maneuvers? About this other bearing I am going to say a very quick word, in order to conclude and try to respond, if possible, to a request. Several times I have been asked (and that is why I shall allow myself a brief galatic ostentation of certain of my writings) why (with a view to what, to what ends, and so on) I had or had *taken on* an apocalyptic tone and put forward apocalyptic themes. That is how they have often been qualified, sometimes with suspicion, and above all, I have noticed, in the United States, where people are always more sensitive to phenomena of prophetism, messianism, eschatology, and apocalypse-here-now. That I have multiplied the distinctions between closure and end, that I was aware of speaking of discourses *on* the end rather than announcing the end, that I intended to analyze a genre rather than practice it, and even when I would practice it, to do so with that ironic genre clause I tried to show never belonged to the genre itself; nevertheless, for the reasons I gave a few minutes ago, all language on apocalypse is also apocalyptic and cannot be excluded from its object. Then I also asked myself why, to what ends, with a view to what, the Apocalypse itself—I mean the historic writings thus named and first the one signed by John of Patmos—had little by little settled in, above all for the last six or seven years, as a theme, a concern, a fascination, an explicit reference, and the horizon for me of work or a task, although I know these rich and secret texts very badly. This was first the case in *Glas,* whose columns are constantly shaken by apocalyptic shocks or laughs on the subject of apocalypse and which, in a certain moment (196), mixes the remains of genres and of John, the John of the Gospel, of the Apocalypse, and of Genet. We see there: "The Gospel and the Apocalypse, violently selected, fragmented, redistributed, with blanks, shifts of accent, lines skipped or moved out of place, as if they reached us over a broken-down teletype, a wiretap [*table d'écoute*] in an overloaded telephone exchange." And a long sequence jumbling the citations to an end thus:

> "And I, John, I have heard and seen all these things." As his name indicates: the apocalyptic, in other words, capital unveiling, in truth lays bare self-hunger. *Funeral Rites,* you recall, on the same page: "Jean was taken away from me. . . . Jean needed a compensation . . . the . . . revelation of my friendship for Jean. . . . I was hungry for Jean." That [*Ça*] is called a colossal compensation. The absolute phantasm as an absolute self-having [*s'avoir absolu*] in its most mournful glory: to engulf (one)self in order to be close-by-(one)self, to make (one)self a mouthful [*bouchée*], to be(come) (in a word, band (erect)) one's own proper bit [*mors*]. [*Glas,* 198]

That was finally, as I said a few minutes ago, the case with *The Post Card,* where the allusions increase to the Apocalypse and to its arithmosophy, where everything speculates on figures and notably seven, the "written, 7," the angels, "my angel," messengers and postmen [*facteurs*], prediction, the announcement of the news, the holocaustic "burning," and all the phenomena of *Verstimmung,* of change of tone, of mixing genres, of *destinerrance,* if I can say that, or of *clandestination,* so many signs of more or less bastard apocalyptic filiation. But it is not this thematic or tonal network that I wanted, in concluding, to stress. For want of time, I shall limit myself to the word, if it is a word, and to the motif "Come" that occupies other texts written in the meantime, in particular "Pas,"[15] "Living On,"[16] and "At This Very Moment in This Work Here I Am,"[17] three texts dedicated, we can say, to Blanchot and to Levinas. I was not immediately aware of the citational resonance of this "Come," or at least that its citation (for the drama of its citationality was what mattered to me at the outset, its repetitive structure and what, even in a tone, must be able to be repeated, thus mimicked, indeed "synthesized") was also a reference to John's Apocalypse. I was not thinking of this when I wrote "Pas," but I did know it at the time of the other two texts. And I noted it. "Come," *erkhou, veni, viens,* this appeal resounds in the heart of the vision, in the "I see" following Christ's dictation (starting from chapter 4) when it is said:

> I see in the right hand of him who is sitting on the throne
> a volume written on the inside and out,
> sealed with seals: seven.
>
> I see a messenger, strong.
> He cries in a great voice:
> "Who is worthy to open the volume,
> and break its seals?"
>
> No one can,
> in heaven, on earth, or under the earth,
> open the volume or look at it.
>
> [5:1–3]

And each time the Lamb opens one of the seven seals, one of the four living says, "Come," and it is the continuation of the Horsemen of the Apocalypse. (In the "Envois" of *The Post Card,* one or the other often says: they will believe that we are two, or that I am alone, or that we are three, or that we are four; and it is not certain that they are wrong; but everything happens as if the hypothesis could not go beyond four; in any case that is the fiction.) Further on—I mean in John's Apocalypse—in chapter 17, one of the seven messengers with the seven cups says, " 'Come. I shall show you the judgment / of the great whore' "[17:1]. It is a question of Babel. And in chapter 21, " 'Come! I shall show you / the bride, the wife of the Lamb' " [21:9]. And above all, at the end of ends, "Come" launches into or echoes itself in an exchange of calls and responses that is precisely no longer an exchange. The voices, the places, the routes of "Come" traverse the partition [*paroi*] of a song, a volume of citational and recitative echoes, as if it [*ça*] began by responding. And in this traversal or this transfer(ence), the voices find their spacing, the space of their movement, but they nullify it with one stroke [*d'un trait*]; they no longer give it time.

There is a kind of general narrator there: at the moment of the signature, he will call himself the witness (*marturōn, testimonium*). There is the angelic messenger there whose *envoi* he reports. There is John there who begins to speak again and says that presently he is prostrating himself before the messenger who speaks to him:

> He tells me:
> "Do not seal the words of the inspiration of this volume:
> yes, the time is near."
>
> [22:10]

Double bind of an order John could only disobey in order to obey. Then Jesus speaks again, naturally in this mode reported live [*ce mode rapporté en direct*] that Plato called mimetic or apocryphal, and the play of quotation marks in the translation poses all the problems you can imagine. Each time we know that so-and-so speaks because he introduces himself; I, so-and-so; but he does this in the text written by the witness or the general narrator who is always a party to it. Here it is, and it is the end:

> "I, Yéshoua', I have sent my messenger
> to testify this to you about the communities.
> I am the scion and the seed of Dawid,
> the shining star of the morning."
>
> [22:16]

Close quote. The text of the witness resumes:

> The breath and the bride (*numphē, sponsa,* the promised) say [together]: "Come."
> Let the hearer say: "Come."
> Let the thirsty come,
> let the volunteer take the water of life, freely.
> I myself testify to every hearer
> of the words of the inspiration of this volume:
> if anyone adds to them,
> Elohim will add to him the afflictions described in this volume.
> If anyone takes away from the words
> of the volume of this inspiration,
> Elohim will take away his share of the tree of life,
> outside the city of the sanctuary described in this volume.
>
> The witness to these things says: "Yes, I come quickly."
> Amen. Come, Adôn Yéshoua'.
> Dilection of the Adôn Yéshoua' to all . . .
>
> [22:17–20]

The event of this "Come" precedes and calls the event. It would be that starting from which there is any event, the coming, the to-come of the event that cannot be thought under the given category of event. "Come" appeared to me to appeal to the "place" (but here the word *place* becomes too enigmatic), let us say to the place, the time, and to the advent of what in the apocalyptic in general no longer lets itself be contained simply by philosophy, metaphysics, onto-eschato-theology, and by all the readings they have proposed of the apocalyptic. I cannot reconstitute what I have attempted in this respect in a milieu of resonances, responses, citations referred, referring to texts of Blanchot, Levinas, Heidegger, or others such as one could hazard to do today with the latest book of Marguerite Duras, *The Seated Man in the Passage.*[18] What I had then tried to expose to an analysis that would be, among other things, a spectrography of tone and of change of tone could not by definition keep itself at the disposal or to the measure of philosophical, pedagogical, or teaching demonstration. First of all, because "Come," opening the scene, could not become an object, a theme, a representation, or indeed a citation in the current sense, and subsumable under a category, even were it that of coming or event. For the same reason, that bends itself with difficulty to the rhetoric required by the present scene. Nevertheless, I am trying to extract from this, at the risk of essentially deforming it, the demonstrative function in terms of philosophical discourse.

Accelerating the movement, I shall then say this. Come from the other already as a response, and a citation without past present, "Come" tolerates no metalinguistic citation, even when it is, "Come" itself, a narrative [*un récit*], already, a recitative and a song whose singularity remains at once absolute and absolutely divisible. "Come" no more lets itself be arraigned [*arraisonner*] by an onto-theo-eschatology than by a logic of the event, however new they may be and whatever politics they announce. In this *affirmative* tone, "Come" marks in itself, in oneself, neither a desire nor an order, neither a prayer nor a request [*demande*]. More precisely, the grammatical, linguistic, or semantic categories from which the "Come" would thus be determined are traversed by the

"Come." This "Come"—I do not know what *it is*, not because I yield to obscurantism, but because the question "what is" belongs to a space (ontology, and from it the knowledge of grammar, linguistics, semantics, and so on) opened by a "come" come from the other. Between all the "come"s, the difference is not grammatical, linguistic, semantic, pragmatic—and which permits saying: it's an imperative, it's a jussive modality, it's a performative of such and such a type, and so on—the difference is tonal. And I do not know whether a tonal difference finally lends itself to all these questions. Try to say "come"—it can be said in every tone, and you'll see, you'll hear, the other will hear first—perhaps or not. It is the gesture in speaking [*parole*], that gesture that does not let itself be recovered [*reprendre*] by the analysis—linguistic, semantic, or rhetorical—of speaking.

Come [*Viens*] beyond being, it, engaging perhaps in the place in which *Ereignis* (no longer can this be translated by "event") and *Enteignis* unfold the movement of propriation, comes from beyond being and calls beyond being. If "Come" does not try to lead, if it no doubt is an-agogic, it can always be led back higher than itself, anagogically, toward conductive violence, toward authoritarian "duction." This risk is ineluctable; it threatens the tone as its double. And even in the confession of seduction: in saying in a certain tone, "I am in the act of seducing you," I do not suspend, I can even increase, the seductive power. Perhaps Heidegger would not have liked this apparently personal conjugation or declension of coming. But such conjugation and declension are not personal, subjective, or egological. "Come" cannot come from a voice or at least not from a tone signifying "I" or "self," a so-and-so (male or female) in my "determination," my *Bestimmung:* vocation to the destination *myself*. "Come" does not address itself to an identity determinable in advance. It is a drift [*une dérive*] underivable from the identity of a determination. "Come" is *only* derivable, absolutely derivable, but only from the other, from nothing that may be an origin or a verifiable, decidable, presentable, appropriable identity, from nothing not already derivable and arrivable without *rive* [bank, shore].

Perhaps you will be tempted to call this disaster, catastrophe, apocalypse. Now here, precisely, is announced—as promise or threat—an apocalypse without apocalypse, an apocalypse without vision, without truth, without revelation, *envois* (for the "Come" is plural in itself, in oneself), addresses without message and without destination, without sender or decidable addressee, without last judgment, without any other eschatology than the tone of the "Come," its very differance, an apocalypse beyond good and evil. "Come" does not announce this or that apocalypse: already it resounds with a certain tone; it is in itself the apocalypse of apocalypse; *Come* is apocalyptic.

Our *apocalypse now:* there would be no more chance, save chance itself, for a thought of good and evil whose announcement would come to *gather* itself in order to be with itself in a revelatory speaking; (no) more chance, unless a chance, the unique, chance itself, for a collection of truth, a *legein* of *alētheia* that would no longer be a legendary unveiling; and (no) more chance even for such a gathering of gift, *envoi,* destiny (*Schicken, Geschick*), for the destination of a "come" whose promise at least would be assured of its own proper event.

But then what is someone doing who says to you: I tell you this, I have come to tell you this, there is not, there has never been, there will never be apocalypse, "the apocalypse is disappointing"? There is the apocalypse *without* apocalypse.

The word *sans,* "without," I pronounce here in the so necessary syntax of Blanchot, who often says *X without X.* The *without* marks an internal and external catastrophe of the apocalypse, an overturning of sense that does not merge with the catastrophe announced or described in the apocalyptic writings without, however, being foreign to them. Here the catastrophe would perhaps be *of* the apocalypse itself, its fold [*pli*] and its end, a closure without end, an end without end.

But what reading, what history of reading, what philology, what hermeneutic competence authorizes one to say that this very thing, this catastrophe *of* the apocalypse, is not the catastrophe described, in its movement and its very course [*trajet*], in its outline [*tracé*], by *this* or *that* apocalyptic writing? For example, the one from Patmos that would then be doomed to going out of itself in this aleatory errance?

And what if this outside of apocalypse were *inside* the apocalypse? What if it were the apocalypse itself, what precisely breaks in [*fait effraction*] in the "Come"? What is "inside" and what is "outside" a text, of *this* text, both inside and outside these volumes of which we do not know whether they are open or closed?

Of this volume written, you remember, "on the inside and out," it is said at the very end: do not seal this; " 'Do not seal the words of the inspiration of this volume. . . .' "

Do not seal, that is to say, do not close, but also do not sign.

The end approaches, now it's too late to tell the truth about the apocalypse. But what are you doing, all of you will still insist, to what ends do you want to come when you come to tell us, here now, let's go, come, the apocalypse, it's finished, I tell you this, that's what's happening.

Notes

Earlier versions of this translation appeared in the journals *Semeia* and *The Oxford Literary Review.* The text in *Semeia* is a translation of the lecture given the last full day of the conference at Cerisy-la-

Salle, France, on the work of Jacques Derrida, or, rather, starting from his work, and published in the proceedings of the conference, Philippe Lacoue-Labarthe and Jean-Luc Nancy, eds., *Les Fins de l'homme. A partir du travail de Jacques Derrida* (Paris: Galilée, 1981). The text in *The Oxford Literary Review* is a translation of the revised version published separately by Editions Galilée in 1983. The present text is a "final" revision of the version in *The Oxford Literary Review* and incorporates Peter Fenves's translation of the Kant text and other translations of Derrida and Blanchot now available.

Convened from 23 July to 2 August 1980, the conference where Derrida's lecture was delivered consisted of lectures, discussions, and seminars on Derrida's effects within diverse perspectives and disciplines. The format of the ten-day gathering explains the references in the text to the organizers, seminars, and some participants—Philippe Lacoue-Labarthe, Jean-Luc Nancy, and Jean Ricardou—as well as to questions left open for discussion following the presentation.

Derrida refers in this text to the translations of André Chouraqui of the Apocalypse of John and other biblical texts. I have translated the biblical texts cited from the French of Chouraqui. I have also consulted *The Four Gospels and the Revelation,* trans. Richmond Lattimore (New York: Farrar, 1962, 1979), for the translations of the Apocalypse. For the Greek text I have used the United Bible Societies Greek New Testament, 2d edition; for the Latin, Wordsworth and White's edition of *Novum Testamentum Latine* according to the edition of St. Jerome (London: Oxford University Press, 1957).

I would like to thank Geoff Bennington for his scrupulous reading of and his corrections and suggestions for improvement of the version that appeared in *The Oxford Literary Review.* And once again I am indebted to Jacques Derrida for his gracious help and patience.

1. *La Bible: Il crie . . . ,* trans. André Chouraqui (Paris; Desclée de Brouwer, 1974).

2. Immanuel Kant, *Von einem neuerdings erhobenen vornehmen Ton in der Philosophie, Kants Gesammelte Schriften,* ed. Royal Prussian (Later, German) Academy of Sciences (Berlin and Leipzig: Walter de Gruyter, 1902–), 8:387–406. Kant's *D'un ton grand seigneur adopté naguère en philosophie,* in his *Première Introduction à la Critique de la faculté de juger,* trans. L. Guillermit (Paris: Vrin, 1975): 87–109—hereafter *D'un ton;* "On a Newly Arisen Superior Tone in Philosophy," trans. Peter Fenves, in this volume. Since the English

translation indicates the Akademie edition's pagination, I give those page numbers exclusively for the German and English references to Kant's text.

3. Jacques Derrida, *Glas,* trans. John P. Leavey, Jr., and Richard Rand (Lincoln: University of Nebraska Press, 1986).

4. Jacques Derrida, *The Post Card: From Socrates to Freud and Beyond,* trans. Alan Bass (Chicago: University of Chicago Press, 1987).

5. Immanuel Kant, *The Conflict of the Faculties,* intro. Mary J. Gregor. trans. Mary J. Gregor and Robert E. Anchor (New York: Abaris, 1979).

6. See Jacques Derrida, "Scribble (writing-power)," trans. Cary Plotkin, *Yale French Studies* 58 (1979): 116–47.

7. Immanuel Kant, *Religion within the Limits of Reason Alone,* trans. Theodore M. Greene and Hoyt H. Hudson (New York: Harper and Row, 1960), 125; 6:134.

8. See Jacques Derrida, *Spurs: Nietzsche's Styles / Eperons: Les Styles de Nietzsche,* trans. Barbara Harlow (Chicago: University of Chicago Press, 1979).

9. Jacques Derrida, "Economimesis," trans. Richard Klein, *Diacritics* 11:2 (Summer 1981): 3–25.

10. Sigmund Freud, "The Infantile Genital Organization: An Interpolation into the Theory of Sexuality (1923)," *The Standard Edition of the Complete Psychological Works of Sigmund Freud,* trans. and ed. James Strachey (London: Hogarth Press and the Institute of Psycho-Analysis, 1961), 19:145.

11. Friedrich Hölderlin and Eduard Mörike, *Selected Poems,* trans. Christopher Middleton (Chicago: University of Chicago Press, 1972), 74–75, 88–89, translation modified.

12. Maurice Blanchot, *The Last Man,* trans. Lydia Davis (New York: Columbia University Press, 1987).

13. Friedrich Nietzsche, *Philosophy and Truth: Selections from Nietzsche's Notebooks of the Early 1870s,* trans. Daniel Breazeale (Atlantic Highlands, N.J.: Humanities Press, 1979), 33–34 (#87); Nietzsche, *Nachgelassene Fragmente: Sommer 1872 bis Ende 1874,* 3:4 of *Nietzsches Werke: Kritische Gesamtausgabe,* ed. Giorgio Colli and Mazzino Montinari (Berlin: de Gruyter, 1978), 48–49.

14. Maurice Blanchot, *The Madness of the Day,* trans. Lydia Davis (Barrytown, N.Y.: Station Hill Press, 1981), 10, 24.

15. Jacques Derrida, "Pas," *Parages* (Paris: Galilée, 1986), 19–116.

16. Jacques Derrida, "Living On," trans. James Hulbert, in *De-*

construction and Criticism (New York: Seabury, 1979), 75–176; Derrida, "Survivre," *Parages,* 117–218.

17. Jacques Derrida, "At This Very Moment in This Work Here I Am," trans. Ruben Berezdivin, in *Re-Reading Levinas,* ed. Robert Bernasconi and Simon Critchley (Bloomington: Indiana University Press, 1991), 11–48.

18. Marguerite Duras, *The Seated Man in the Passage,* trans. Mary Lydon, *Contemporary Literature* 24:2 (1983): 268–75.

Index

Designed by Julie Burris

Composed by Graphic Composition, Inc.,
in Baskerville text and display

Printed by The Maple Press Company, Inc.,
on 55-lb. Sebago Antique Cream, and bound in
Roxite vellum finish cloth